most
loved

appetizers

Pictured on Front Cover:

Chili Lemon Shrimp, page 64

Pictured on Back Cover:

1. Mushroom Turnovers, page 66
2. Beefy Pepper Dim Sum, page 104
3. Baby Cheddar Tarts, page 97
4. Zippy Canapés, page 58
5. Curried Chicken Rolls, page 102
6. Toast Cups, page 31,
   with Antipasto, page 46

Sixth Printing December 2006

Library and Archives Canada Cataloguing in Publication

Paré, Jean, date.
Most loved appetizers / Jean Paré.
(Most loved recipe collection)
Includes index.
ISBN 978-1-896891-70-5
1. Appetizers. I. Title. II. Series.
TX740.P36 2003   641.8'12   C2003-902093-2

Published by
Company's Coming Publishing Limited
2311 – 96 Street
Edmonton, Alberta, Canada T6N 1G3
Tel: 780-450-6223   Fax: 780-450-1857
www.companyscoming.com

Company's Coming is a registered trademark owned by Company's Coming Publishing Limited

Printed in China

We gratefully acknowledge the following suppliers for their generous support of our Test and Photography Kitchens:

Corelle®
Lagostina®
Tupperware®

Our special thanks to the following businesses for providing props for photography:

Anchor Hocking Canada
Browne & Co. Ltd.
Canhome Global
Cherison Enterprises Inc.
Chintz & Company
Danesco Inc.
Exquisite Sewing Centre
Island Pottery Inc.
La Cache
Le Gnome
Mikasa Home Store
Pfaltzgraff Canada
Scona Clayworks
Stokes
The Bay

Pictured from left: Sesame Sticks, page 11; Bruschetta, page 90; Shrimp Salad Wraps, page 82; Jalapeño Cheese, page 24

table of contents

the Company's Coming story

"never share a recipe you wouldn't use yourself"

Jean Paré (pronounced "jeen PAIR-ee") grew up understanding that the combination of family, friends and home cooking is the best recipe for a good life. From her mother, she learned to appreciate good cooking, while her father praised even her earliest attempts in the kitchen. When Jean left home, she took with her a love of cooking, many family recipes and an intriguing desire to read cookbooks as if they were novels!

In 1963, when her four children had all reached school age, Jean volunteered to cater the 50th Anniversary of the Vermilion School of Agriculture, now Lakeland College, in Alberta, Canada. Working out of her home, Jean prepared a dinner for more than 1,000 people, which launched a flourishing catering operation that continued for over 18 years. During that time, she had countless opportunities to test new ideas with immediate feedback—resulting in empty plates and contented customers! Whether preparing cocktail sandwiches for a house party or serving a hot meal for 1,500 people, Jean Paré earned a reputation for good food, courteous service and reasonable prices.

As requests for her recipes mounted, Jean was often asked the question, "Why don't you write a cookbook?" Jean responded by teaming up with her son, Grant Lovig, in the fall of 1980 to form Company's Coming Publishing Limited. The publication of *150 Delicious Squares* on April 14, 1981 marked the debut of what would soon become one of the world's most popular cookbook series.

The company has grown since those early days when Jean worked from a spare bedroom in her home. Today, she continues to write recipes while working closely with the staff of the Recipe Factory, as the Company's Coming test kitchen is affectionately known. There she fills the role of mentor, assisting with the development of recipes people most want to use for everyday cooking and easy entertaining. Every Company's Coming recipe is *kitchen-tested* before it's approved for publication.

Jean's daughter, Gail Lovig, is responsible for marketing and distribution, leading a team that includes sales personnel located in major cities across Canada. In addition, Company's Coming cookbooks are published and distributed under licence in the United States, Australia and other world markets. Bestsellers many times over in English, Company's Coming cookbooks have also been published in French and Spanish.

Familiar and trusted in home kitchens around the world, Company's Coming cookbooks are offered in a variety of formats. Highly regarded as kitchen workbooks, the softcover Original Series, with its lay-flat plastic comb binding, is still a favourite among readers.

Jean Paré's approach to cooking has always called for *quick and easy recipes* using *everyday ingredients.* That view has served her well. The recipient of many awards, including the Queen Elizabeth Golden Jubilee medal, Jean was appointed a Member of the Order of Canada, her country's highest lifetime achievement honour.

Jean continues to gain new supporters by adhering to what she calls The Golden Rule of Cooking: *"Never share a recipe you wouldn't use yourself."* It's an approach that works— *millions of times over!*

foreword

Most Loved Appetizers brings together more than two decades of our very best appetizer recipes. With this handy book on your shelf, you'll never be caught without something to make for your guests.

Serving appetizers is an easy way to get a party started and to get the conversation flowing. Tasty morsels can whet the appetite for the meal to follow or simply satisfy the munchies over cocktails. In *Most Loved Appetizers*, we've included everything from our old favourites, such as Surprise Spread, page 6, to some of our more recent hits.

Contrary to popular belief, appetizers don't have to be fussy to make. Many delicious starters can be created with a minimum amount of ingredients and time. We've also suggested some additional time savers and make ahead tips.

One of the best things about appetizers is that they offer new and experienced cooks the opportunity to be adventuresome. Let your imagination run wild and have fun experimenting with different shapes, sizes and, above all, flavours. These savoury snacks can be as much fun to make as they are to eat!

When preparing appetizers, remember that visual appeal is a must—they should be small and inviting. Experiment with a variety of textures, colours and tastes; serve them hot or cold, simple or elegant. If you are throwing a large party, you might want to invest in some decorative cocktail picks and platters. The preparation can be time-consuming but worth the effort!

Turn the great results that you will achieve with *Most Loved Appetizers* into a great beginning for your next cocktail party, baby shower, office gathering or community event. With this collection of treasured treats, you can kick off any gathering with style—and you'll always be ready when company's coming!

Jean Paré

nutrition information

Each recipe has been analyzed using the most up-to-date version of the Canadian Nutrient File from Health Canada, which is based on the United States Department of Agriculture (USDA) Nutrient Data Base. If more than one ingredient is listed (such as "hard margarine or butter"), then the first ingredient is used in the analysis. Where an ingredient reads "sprinkle," "optional," or "for garnish," it is not included as part of the nutrition information.

Margaret Ng, B.Sc. (Hon.), M.A.
Registered Dietitian

You'll be tempted to eat this very popular spread by the spoonful. Everybody loves this one! It shows up at party, after party, after party....

note

An economical substitution for 3 cans of small shrimp is 2 1/4 cups (550 mL) frozen small shrimp, thawed.

dippers

Assorted tortilla chips, Toast Points, page 31

Surprise Spread

Block of cream cheese, softened	8 oz.	250 g
Sour cream	1/2 cup	125 mL
Salad dressing (or mayonnaise)	1/4 cup	60 mL
Cans of small shrimp (4 oz., 113 g, each), rinsed and drained (see Note, this page)	3	3
Seafood cocktail sauce	1 cup	250 mL
Grated mozzarella cheese	2 cups	500 mL
Medium green pepper, chopped	1	1
Green onions, chopped	3	3
Medium tomato, diced	1	1

Combine cream cheese, sour cream and salad dressing in small bowl. Spread in ungreased 12 inch (30 cm) pizza pan or on serving platter.

Scatter shrimp over cream cheese mixture.

Layer remaining 5 ingredients, in order given, over shrimp. Cover. Chill until ready to serve. Serves 10 to 12.

1 serving: 286 Calories; 21.4 g Total Fat (7.3 g Mono, 2.4 g Poly, 10.4 g Sat); 107 mg Cholesterol; 9 g Carbohydrate; 1 g Fibre; 14 g Protein; 572 mg Sodium

Pictured on page 7.

If you like things hot, add more cayenne pepper to this dip. It has a pleasant flavour and an attractive browned top.

dippers

Tortilla Chips, page 10, Tortilla Crisps, page 10

black bean dip

Substitute 2 cans of black beans (19 oz., 540 mL, each), rinsed and drained, for the kidney beans.

Kidney Bean Dip

BOTTOM LAYER

Cans of kidney beans (14 oz., 398 mL, each), drained	2	2
Sliced green onion	1/2 cup	125 mL
Salsa	6 tbsp.	100 mL
Parsley flakes	2 tsp.	10 mL
White vinegar	1 tsp.	5 mL
Chili powder	1 tsp.	5 mL
Onion powder	1/2 tsp.	2 mL
Salt	1/2 tsp.	2 mL
Cayenne pepper	1/4 tsp.	1 mL
Garlic powder	1/4 tsp.	1 mL

TOP LAYER

Grated medium Cheddar cheese	1 cup	250 mL
Grated Monterey Jack cheese	1 cup	250 mL
Chili powder	1 tsp.	5 mL

Bottom Layer: Mash kidney beans with fork in medium bowl.

Add next 9 ingredients. Mix well. Spread in ungreased 9 inch (22 cm) pie plate or shallow casserole.

Top Layer: Layer all 3 ingredients, in order given, over salsa mixture. Bake, uncovered, in 350°F (175°C) oven for 30 minutes. Makes about 4 cups (1 L).

2 tbsp. (30 mL): 48 Calories; 2.4 g Total Fat (0.7 g Mono, 0.1 g Poly, 1.5 g Sat); 7 mg Cholesterol; 4 g Carbohydrate; 1 g Fibre; 3 g Protein; 158 mg Sodium

Pictured on page 9.

Top Centre: Tortilla Crisps, page 10
Top Right: Tortilla Chips, page 10
Bottom: Kidney Bean Dip, above

These are so easy to make and the result is very tasty.

serving suggestion

Serve as a dipper for Mexican-type dips, such as Kidney Bean Dip, page 8, and Refried Bean Dip, page 52.

Tortilla Crisps

Hard margarine (or butter), softened	3/4 cup	175 mL
Grated Parmesan cheese	1/2 cup	125 mL
Sesame seeds	1/4 cup	60 mL
Parsley flakes	2 tsp.	10 mL
Dried whole oregano	1/2 tsp.	2 mL
Onion powder	1/4 tsp.	1 mL
Garlic powder	1/4 tsp.	1 mL
Flour tortillas (6 inch, 15 cm, diameter)	12	12

Combine first 7 ingredients in small bowl.

Divide and spread thick layer of Parmesan cheese mixture on each tortilla. It will seem like too much but once cooked they will be just right. Cut each tortilla into 8 wedges. Arrange in single layer on ungreased baking sheets. Bake in 350°F (175°C) oven for 12 to 15 minutes until crisp and golden. Makes 96 crisps.

4 crisps: 129 Calories; 7.8 g Total Fat (4.5 g Mono, 1.1 g Poly, 1.8 g Sat); 2 mg Cholesterol; 12 g Carbohydrate; trace Fibre; 3 g Protein; 182 mg Sodium

Pictured on page 9.

The wonderful thing about these appetizers is that you can deep-fry or bake them—either way they're delicious!

oven tortilla chips

Arrange tortilla wedges in single layer on ungreased baking sheets. Brush lightly with water. Sprinkle with salt. Bake in 400°F (205°C) oven for 8 minutes. Turn wedges over. Bake for about 3 minutes until crisp and golden.

Tortilla Chips

Corn tortillas (6 inch, 15 cm, diameter)	12	12
Cooking oil, for deep-frying		

Salt (or seasoned salt), sprinkle

Cut each tortilla into 8 wedges. Deep-fry, several at a time, in hot (375°F, 190°C) cooking oil, turning occasionally, until crisp. Remove to paper towels to drain.

Sprinkle with salt. Makes 96 chips.

4 chips: 72 Calories; 3.8 g Total Fat (1.8 g Mono, 0.9 g Poly, 0.2 g Sat); 0 mg Cholesterol; 9 g Carbohydrate; 1 g Fibre; 1 g Protein; 35 mg Sodium

Pictured on page 9.

Sesame Sticks

Mashed potatoes	1 cup	250 mL
Hard margarine (or butter), softened	1/2 cup	125 mL
Seasoned salt	1/4 tsp.	1 mL
All-purpose flour	1 cup	250 mL
Large egg, fork-beaten	1	1
Water	1 tbsp.	15 mL
Salt	1/2 tsp.	2 mL
Sesame seeds	4 tsp.	20 mL

Combine potatoes, margarine and seasoned salt in medium bowl.

Add flour. Mix well. Chill for several hours or overnight for ease of handling. Roll out on lightly floured surface to 1/4 inch (6 mm) thickness.

Mix egg and water in cup. Brush over top.

Sprinkle with salt and sesame seeds. Cut into 4 inch (10 cm) strips, about 1/2 inch (12 mm) wide. Transfer carefully with lifter to greased baking sheet. Bake in 400°F (205°C) oven for about 20 minutes until crisp and golden. Makes 34 bread sticks.

2 bread sticks: 100 Calories; 6.5 g Total Fat (4 g Mono, 0.8 g Poly, 1.3 g Sat); 13 mg Cholesterol; 9 g Carbohydrate; 1 g Fibre; 2 g Protein; 173 mg Sodium

Pictured on this page.

The crispy exterior has a delicious buttery, nutty flavour.

serving suggestion

Serve as a dipper for your favourite sauce or as an accompaniment to soup.

Serve this special dip hot from the oven and watch it disappear. It will become a regular at all your gatherings.

dippers

Assorted crackers, assorted tortilla chips

double devil's dip

Add 2 tbsp. (30 mL) chili powder to the first 6 ingredients. Mix well.

Devil's Dip

Block of cream cheese, softened	8 oz.	250 g
Sour cream	1 cup	250 mL
Can of jalapeño bean dip	10 1/2 oz.	298 g
Drops of hot pepper sauce	10	10
Dried chives	3 tbsp.	50 mL
Parsley flakes	2 tsp.	10 mL
Chili powder	1 tsp.	5 mL
Grated Monterey Jack cheese	1 1/2 cups	375 mL
Grated medium Cheddar cheese	1 1/2 cups	375 mL
Chili powder, sprinkle		
Pickled jalapeño pepper slices, for garnish		

Put first 6 ingredients into medium bowl. Mix well. Spread in ungreased 9 x 13 inch (22 x 33 cm) pan.

Layer next 4 ingredients, in order given, over bean dip mixture. Bake in 350°F (175°C) oven for 20 to 40 minutes until crispy.

Garnish with jalapeño pepper slices. Makes 4 cups (1 L).

2 tbsp. (30 mL): 92 Calories; 7.2 g Total Fat (2.1 g Mono, 0.3 g Poly, 4.5 g Sat); 22 mg Cholesterol; 3 g Carbohydrate; trace Fibre; 4 g Protein; 118 mg Sodium

Pictured on page 13.

This classic appetizer is a true favourite.

make ahead

Make several days ahead. Double to make 1 larger ball or to make 2—1 for the freezer and 1 to chill for tomorrow's party.

Sauced Crab Ball

Block of cream cheese, softened	4 oz.	125 g
Can of crabmeat, drained and cartilage removed, flaked	4 oz.	113 g
Lemon juice	1 tsp.	5 mL
Onion powder	1/4 tsp.	1 mL
Hot pepper sauce, dash		
Seafood cocktail sauce	1/3 cup	75 mL
Chopped fresh chives, for garnish		

(continued on next page)

Put first 5 ingredients into small bowl. Beat until well combined. Shape into ball. Cover. Chill. Makes about 1 cup (250 mL).

Just before serving, place on serving plate. Pour cocktail sauce over crab ball. Garnish with chives. Add more cocktail sauce as needed. Serves 8.

1 serving: *71 Calories; 5.4 g Total Fat (1.5 g Mono, 0.2 g Poly, 3.3 g Sat); 16 mg Cholesterol; 3 g Carbohydrate; trace Fibre; 3 g Protein; 256 mg Sodium*

Pictured below.

Top: Devil's Dip, page 12
Bottom Right: Sauced Crab Ball, page 12

dippers

Assorted crackers

homemade cocktail sauce

Combine 1/4 cup (60 mL) ketchup, 1 – 2 tsp. (5 – 10 mL) prepared horseradish and 1 tsp. (5 mL) lemon juice in small bowl. Chill for 1 hour. Makes 1/4 cup (60 mL) sauce. Easily doubled or tripled.

A sweet vegetable dip. Use half and freeze half of this large recipe so that it's ready at a moment's notice.

note

Dark corn syrup adds a bit more colour than light corn syrup but either can be used.

make ahead

Freeze for up to 6 months.

presentation idea

Cut carrots and cucumbers with a crinkle cutter to make ruffled edges. Use a citrus stripper to create "stripes" on radishes, mushrooms, cucumbers, oranges and lemons.

Best Vegetable Dip

Block of cream cheese, softened	8 oz.	250 g
Dark corn syrup (see Note, this page)	1/2 cup	125 mL
Granulated sugar	1/2 cup	125 mL
Cooking oil	1 cup	250 mL
White vinegar	1/4 cup	60 mL
Minced onion flakes	1/4 cup	60 mL
Lemon juice	1 tbsp.	15 mL
Dry mustard	1 tsp.	5 mL
Celery seed	1 tsp.	5 mL
Salt	1/2 tsp.	2 mL
Paprika	1/4 tsp.	1 mL

Put cream cheese, corn syrup and sugar into medium bowl. Beat until well combined.

Add cooking oil. Mix.

Add remaining 7 ingredients. Beat until combined. Chill until ready to serve. Makes 3 cups (750 mL).

2 tbsp. (30 mL): 156 Calories; 12.8 g Total Fat (6.5 g Mono, 2.9 g Poly, 2.9 g Sat); 11 mg Cholesterol; 11 g Carbohydrate; trace Fibre; 1 g Protein; 86 mg Sodium

Pictured on page 15.

This wonderful sauce has a bite that lingers!

dippers

Spring Rolls, page 88, Green Onion Cakes, page 116, Pot Stickers, page 118

Spicy Dipping Sauce

Apple juice	1/2 cup	125 mL
Soy sauce	2 tbsp.	30 mL
Red wine vinegar	2 tbsp.	30 mL
Chili sauce	1 tbsp.	15 mL
Garlic cloves, minced (or 1/2 tsp., 2 mL, powder)	2	2
Dried crushed chilies, finely crushed	1 tsp.	5 mL
Granulated sugar	1/4 tsp.	1 mL
Pepper	1/16 tsp.	0.5 mL

Combine all 8 ingredients in small saucepan. Bring to a simmer on medium-low. Cover. Simmer for 10 minutes. Serve at room temperature. Makes 1/3 cup (75 mL).

1 tbsp. (15 mL): 23 Calories; 0.1 g Total Fat (0 g Mono, trace Poly, trace Sat); 0 mg Cholesterol; 5 g Carbohydrate; trace Fibre; 1 g Protein; 425 mg Sodium

Pictured on page 17.

Very quick to make. It will be gone before it cools!

dippers

Assorted crackers, potato chips, Toast Triangles, page 31

serving suggestion

Transfer hot dip from pie plate to chafing dish to keep warm, or assemble in an attractive shallow stoneware dish and serve straight from oven. Be sure to set it on a trivet!

Hot Crab Dip

Block of cream cheese, softened	8 oz.	250 g
Cans of crabmeat (4 oz., 113 g, each), drained and cartilage removed, flaked	2	2
Finely chopped onion	2 tbsp.	30 mL
Milk	2 tbsp.	30 mL
Creamed horseradish	1/2 tsp.	2 mL
Salt	1/4 tsp.	1 mL
Pepper	1/16 tsp.	0.5 mL
Sliced almonds	1/3 cup	75 mL

Put cream cheese and crab into medium bowl. Mash well.

Add next 5 ingredients. Mix well. Spread in ungreased 9 inch (22 cm) pie plate.

Sprinkle with almonds. Bake in 375°F (190°C) oven for about 15 minutes until heated through. Makes 2 cups (500 mL).

2 tbsp. (30 mL): 76 Calories; 6.5 g Total Fat (2.2 g Mono, 0.4 g Poly, 3.4 g Sat); 17 mg Cholesterol; 1 g Carbohydrate; trace Fibre; 4 g Protein; 170 mg Sodium

Pictured on page 17.

Dilly Dip

Salad dressing (or mayonnaise)	1 cup	250 mL
Sour cream	1 cup	250 mL
Onion flakes	2 tsp.	10 mL
Parsley flakes	2 tsp.	10 mL
Dill weed	2 tsp.	10 mL
Seasoned salt	1 tsp.	5 mL

Chopped fresh dill, for garnish

Mix first 6 ingredients in small bowl. Chill until ready to serve.

Just before serving, transfer to serving bowl. Sprinkle with dill. Makes 2 cups (500 mL).

2 tbsp. (30 mL): 125 Calories; 13.3 g Total Fat (6.8 g Mono, 3.8 g Poly, 2.3 g Sat); 14 mg Cholesterol; 1 g Carbohydrate; trace Fibre; 1 g Protein; 150 mg Sodium

Pictured below.

A classic recipe for one of the best all around dips you will find! A good spur-of-the-moment choice.

dippers

Bread sticks, fresh vegetables (such as baby carrots, broccoli florets, cauliflower florets, celery sticks, cherry or grape tomatoes, radishes, whole mushrooms), potato chips

Top Left: Dilly Dip, this page
Top Right: Hot Crab Dip, page 16
Bottom: Spicy Dipping Sauce, page 16

A block of cream cheese is marinated in soy sauce, ginger and green onion. Very yummy!

note

To toast sesame seeds, spread evenly in ungreased shallow pan. Bake in 350°F (175°C) oven for 5 to 10 minutes, stirring or shaking often, until desired doneness.

time saver

Cut block of cream cheese in half horizontally. Marinate both halves in refrigerator for only 12 hours (or up to 24 hours).

Oriental Cheese Spread

Soy sauce	1/2 cup	125 mL
Icing (confectioner's) sugar	1/4 cup	60 mL
Finely chopped green onion	3 tbsp.	50 mL
Minced crystallized ginger	1 1/2 tbsp.	25 mL
Dried crushed chilies	1 tsp.	5 mL
Garlic clove, minced (or 1/4 tsp., 1 mL, powder)	1	1
Block of cream cheese	8 oz.	250 g
Sesame seeds, toasted (see Note, this page)	3 tbsp.	50 mL

Put first 6 ingredients into small bowl. Stir until icing sugar is dissolved. Pour into resealable freezer bag. Makes 3/4 cup (175 mL) marinade.

Add cream cheese block. Seal bag. Turn until coated. Marinate in refrigerator for 3 days, turning occasionally.

Drain and discard marinade. Spread sesame seeds on waxed paper or large plate. Press cream cheese block into sesame seeds until completely coated. Place on serving plate. Sprinkle any remaining sesame seeds over top. Serves 8 to 10.

1 serving: 138 Calories; 12.6 g Total Fat (3.7 g Mono, 1.1 g Poly, 7.1 g Sat); 34 mg Cholesterol; 3 g Carbohydrate; 1 g Fibre; 3 g Protein; 367 mg Sodium

Pictured below.

Caramel Fruit Dip

Sour cream	1 cup	250 mL
Brown sugar, packed	1 tbsp.	15 mL
Coffee-flavoured liqueur (such as Kahlúa)	1 tbsp.	15 mL

Caramel sauce, for garnish

Combine first 3 ingredients in small bowl.

Drizzle with caramel sauce. Makes 1 cup (250 mL).

2 tbsp. (30 mL): 57 Calories; 4.1 g Total Fat (1.2 g Mono, 0.2 g Poly, 2.5 g Sat); 11 mg Cholesterol; 4 g Carbohydrate; 0 g Fibre; 1 g Protein; 13 mg Sodium

Pictured on page 20.

Easy Fruit Dip

Plain yogurt	1 cup	250 mL
Icing (confectioner's) sugar	3 tbsp.	50 mL
Finely grated lemon zest	1/2 tsp.	2 mL

Combine all 3 ingredients in small bowl. Makes 1 cup (250 mL).

2 tbsp. (30 mL): 30 Calories; 0.5 g Total Fat (0.1 g Mono, trace Poly, 0.3 g Sat); 2 mg Cholesterol; 5 g Carbohydrate; trace Fibre; 2 g Protein; 22 mg Sodium

Pictured on page 21.

Peanut Butter Dip

Smooth peanut butter	1 cup	250 mL
Vanilla ice cream, softened	2 cups	500 mL

Chopped peanuts, for garnish

Measure peanut butter and ice cream into medium bowl. Mix until ice cream is melted and well blended.

Sprinkle with peanuts. Serve immediately. Makes 2 1/2 cups (625 mL).

2 tbsp. (30 mL): 105 Calories; 8.2 g Total Fat (3.6 g Mono, 1.9 g Poly, 2.3 g Sat); 6 mg Cholesterol; 6 g Carbohydrate; 1 g Fibre; 4 g Protein; 72 mg Sodium

Pictured on page 20/21.

These fruit dips will make an excellent trio on your table. Surround them with a gigantic platter of fruit and let your guests enjoy the varied flavours. These dips are so easy to make and can easily be doubled.

dippers

Fresh fruit (such as apple wedges tossed in lemon juice, banana chunks tossed in lemon juice, cantaloupe pieces, Cape gooseberries, fresh pineapple pieces, grapes, honeydew pieces, kiwifruit pieces, orange segments, watermelon chunks, whole strawberries)

variations

Omit the liqueur in the Caramel Fruit Dip if you prefer and double the amount of brown sugar.

For less tang in the Easy Fruit Dip, use only 1/4 tsp. (1 mL) grated lemon zest.

Provide cocktail picks and a shallow dish with 1 cup (250 mL) crushed peanuts along with the Peanut Butter Dip for those who would like to dip and roll!

Relish is a tasty addition to a cheese ball. The two flavours complement each other nicely—like a cheese sandwich and a dill pickle!

make ahead

Make 1 or 2 days ahead to allow flavours to blend, or make 2 smaller balls and freeze 1 for later use.

dippers

Assorted crackers

Try this versatile spread or dip the next time you entertain.

serving suggestion

This recipe is thick enough to serve as a spread with dark cocktail-size bread slices or as a dip with a selection of fresh vegetables.

Relish Cheese Ball

Blocks of light cream cheese (8 oz., 250 g, each), softened	2	2
Grated medium Cheddar cheese	2 cups	500 mL
Sweet pickle relish, drained	1/2 cup	125 mL
Onion powder	1/8 tsp.	0.5 mL
Finely chopped pecans (or walnuts)	1 cup	250 mL

Put first 4 ingredients into medium bowl. Beat on low until well mixed. Shape into ball. If too soft to shape into ball, chill for at least 1 hour.

Roll ball in pecans until coated. Chill for at least 1 hour. Makes 1 cheese ball, 3 1/2 cups (875 mL).

2 tbsp. (30 mL): 100 Calories; 8.5 g Total Fat (3.5 g Mono, 0.9 g Poly, 3.6 g Sat); 17 mg Cholesterol; 2 g Carbohydrate; trace Fibre; 4 g Protein; 232 mg Sodium

Pictured on page 23.

Cuke Spread 'R Dip

Block of light cream cheese, softened	8 oz.	250 g
Peeled, seeded and finely chopped cucumber	2 cups	500 mL
Seasoned salt	1 tsp.	5 mL
Cayenne pepper	1/16 tsp.	0.5 mL

Mash cream cheese with fork in medium bowl.

Add cucumber, seasoned salt and cayenne pepper. Mix well. Chill for at least 2 hours to blend flavours. Makes 3 cups (750 mL).

2 tbsp. (30 mL): 22 Calories; 1.7 g Total Fat (0.5 g Mono, 0.1 g Poly, 0.9 g Sat); 5 mg Cholesterol; 1 g Carbohydrate; trace Fibre; 1 g Protein; 150 mg Sodium

Pictured on page 23.

Pictured on Previous Page:
Top Left: Caramel Fruit Dip, page 19
Top Right: Easy Fruit Dip, page 19
Centre: Peanut Butter Dip, page 19

Top Left: Relish Cheese Ball, above
Centre Right: Cuke Spread 'R Dip, above

Hah-lah-PEH-nyoh jelly is a unique, tasty spread. Its clear, shimmery look is like a jewel on the table.

jalapeño cheese

Place block of cream cheese, or turn out a tub of spreadable cream cheese, onto shallow plate. Cover with Jalapeño Jelly, this page. Serve with a variety of crackers and provide a cocktail spreader.

Pictured on this page.

Jalapeño Jelly

Chopped pickled jalapeño pepper	1/4 cup	60 mL
Chopped red pepper	3/4 cup	175 mL
White vinegar	1 cup	250 mL
Lemon juice	3 tbsp.	50 mL
Granulated sugar	5 cups	1.25 L
Pouch of liquid pectin	3 oz.	85 mL

Put jalapeño and red pepper into blender. Add 1⁄2 of vinegar. Process until smooth. Pour into large saucepan.

Add remaining vinegar, lemon juice and sugar. Bring to a rolling boil on medium-high, stirring often. Boil, uncovered, for 3 minutes.

Add pectin. Stir. Bring to a rolling boil. Boil, uncovered, for 1 minute. Remove from heat. Skim off foam. Pour into sterilized half-pint (250 mL) jars to within 1/4 inch (6 mm) of top. Place sterilized metal lids on jars and screw metal bands on securely. For added assurance against spoilage, process in boiling water bath for 15 minutes. Makes 4 half-pint (250 mL) jars.

2 tbsp. (30 mL): 130 Calories; trace Total Fat (0 g Mono, 0 g Poly, 0 g Sat); 0 mg Cholesterol; 34 g Carbohydrate; trace Fibre; trace Protein; 16 mg Sodium

Pictured below.

Mint Papaya Salsa

Medium papayas, peeled, seeded and diced	2	2
Finely diced red onion	1/2 cup	125 mL
Chopped fresh mint leaves	1/4 cup	60 mL
Lime juice	2 tsp.	10 mL
Salt	1/4 tsp.	1 mL
Pepper, sprinkle		

Combine all 6 ingredients in medium bowl. Cover. Chill for at least 2 hours to blend flavours. Makes 3 cups (750 mL).

2 tbsp. (30 mL): 11 Calories; trace Total Fat (trace Mono, trace Poly, trace Sat); 0 mg Cholesterol; 3 g Carbohydrate; trace Fibre; trace Protein; 28 mg Sodium

Pictured below.

An excellent make-ahead salsa for your next barbecue bash.

make ahead

Keep a supply in refrigerator for up to 5 days.

Both of these very popular dips can be served at room temperature in a small bowl or heated in the Bread Bowl, described below.

bread bowl

Cut top from round or oblong bread loaf. Remove bread from inside, leaving about 1 inch (2.5 cm) thick shell. Reserve removed bread for dipping. Fill hollowed loaf with your choice of either Spinach Dip. Replace top. (You may need to double the recipe if loaf is large.) Wrap filled loaf in foil. Bake in 300°F (150°C) oven for 2 hours. Remove from oven and turn foil back. Remove top.

dippers

Fresh vegetables, reserved bread chunks

variation

To reduce fat, use lower-fat versions of the dairy products.

Spinach Dip #1

Salad dressing (or mayonnaise)	1/2 cup	125 mL
Blocks of cream cheese (8 oz., 250 g, each), softened	2	2
Grated medium Cheddar cheese	1 cup	250 mL
Box of frozen chopped spinach, thawed, drained and squeezed dry	10 oz.	300 g
Bacon slices, cooked crisp and crumbled	6	6
Finely chopped onion	1/4 cup	60 mL
Dill weed	2 tsp.	10 mL
Garlic powder	1/4 tsp.	1 mL
Grated medium Cheddar cheese, for garnish		
Chopped cooked bacon, for garnish		

Beat salad dressing and cream cheese in medium bowl until smooth.

Add next 6 ingredients. Mix well.

Garnish with Cheddar cheese and bacon. Makes 3 cups (750 mL).

2 tbsp. (30 mL): *126 Calories; 11.8 g Total Fat (4.1 g Mono, 1.2 g Poly, 5.9 g Sat); 30 mg Cholesterol; 2 g Carbohydrate; trace Fibre; 4 g Protein; 152 mg Sodium*

Pictured on page 27.

Spinach Dip #2

Box of frozen chopped spinach, thawed, drained and squeezed dry	10 oz.	300 g
Sour cream	1 cup	250 mL
Salad dressing (or mayonnaise)	1 cup	250 mL
Chopped green onion	1/2 cup	125 mL
Parsley flakes	1 tsp.	5 mL
Lemon juice	1 tsp.	5 mL
Seasoned salt	1/2 tsp.	2 mL
Green onion slices, for garnish		
Paprika, sprinkle		

(continued on next page)

Put spinach, sour cream and salad dressing into medium bowl. Stir.

Add next 4 ingredients. Mix well. Chill until ready to serve.

Garnish with green onion slices. Sprinkle with paprika. Serve warm or at room temperature. Makes about 3 cups (750 mL).

2 tbsp. (30 mL): *86 Calories; 8.9 g Total Fat (4.5 g Mono, 2.6 g Poly, 1.6 g Sat); 9 mg Cholesterol; 1 g Carbohydrate; trace Fibre; 1 g Protein; 84 mg Sodium*

Pictured below.

Top Right: Spinach Dip # 2, page 26
Bottom Left: Spinach Dip #1, page 26

It only takes 30 minutes to assemble and bake this exceptionally good dip. Everybody loves this one!

note

To toast almonds, spread evenly in ungreased shallow pan. Bake in 350°F (175°C) oven for 5 to 10 minutes, stirring or shaking often, until desired doneness.

dippers

Baguette slices, French bread chunks, pita wedges, potato chips

The spicy soy flavour that dominates this hot dip goes well with Spring Rolls, page 88, Green Onion Cakes, page 116, and Pot Stickers, page 118.

note

To toast sesame seeds, spread evenly in ungreased shallow pan. Bake in 350°F (175°C) oven for 5 to 10 minutes, stirring or shaking often, until desired doneness.

Artichoke Dip

Can of artichoke hearts, drained and finely chopped	14 oz.	398 mL
Salad dressing (or mayonnaise)	3/4 cup	175 mL
Sour cream	1/4 cup	60 mL
Grated Parmesan cheese	1/2 cup	125 mL
Onion salt	1/16 tsp.	0.5 mL
Garlic powder	1/16 tsp.	0.5 mL
Hot pepper sauce	1/16 tsp.	0.5 mL
Sliced almonds, toasted (see Note, this page)	1/2 cup	125 mL
Paprika	1/2 tsp.	2 mL

Mix first 7 ingredients well in medium bowl. Turn into ungreased 9 inch (22 cm) pie plate. Bake, uncovered, in 350°F (175°C) oven for 15 to 20 minutes until hot.

Sprinkle with almonds and paprika. Makes 2 cups (500 mL).

2 tbsp. (30 mL): 96 Calories; 8.1 g Total Fat (4.3 g Mono, 2.1 g Poly, 1.4 g Sat); 7 mg Cholesterol; 4 g Carbohydrate; 1 g Fibre; 2 g Protein; 173 mg Sodium

Pictured on page 29.

Soy Fire Dip

Soy sauce	1/4 cup	60 mL
Apple cider vinegar	2 tbsp.	30 mL
Ketchup	2 tsp.	10 mL
Garlic clove (or 1/4 tsp., 1 mL, powder)	1	1
Dried crushed chilies	1 tsp.	5 mL
Sesame seeds, toasted (see Note, this page), for garnish		

Process first 5 ingredients in blender until smooth. Transfer to serving bowl. Let stand at room temperature for about 1 hour to blend flavours.

Garnish with sesame seeds. Makes 1/2 cup (125 mL).

2 tbsp. (30 mL): 19 Calories; 0.1 g Total Fat (0 g Mono, 0 g Poly, 0 g Sat); 0 mg Cholesterol; 3 g Carbohydrate; trace Fibre; 2 g Protein; 1091 mg Sodium

Pictured on page 29.

Top: Artichoke Dip, above
Bottom: Soy Fire Dip, above

An easy-to-make spread that will become a winter favourite. One of those deceptively delicious recipes that you can't judge by reading the recipe—you must try it.

note

If you are unable to find the 6 1/2 oz. (184 g) can of corned beef, this size is equivalent to 3/4 cup (175 mL) flaked corned beef.

serving suggestion

Serve with assorted crackers, Toast Cups, page 31, or Toast Points, page 31.

Corned Beef Mousse

Envelope of unflavoured gelatin (equivalent to 1 tbsp., 15 mL)	1	1
Cold water	1/4 cup	60 mL
Can of condensed cream of mushroom soup	10 oz.	284 mL
Block of cream cheese, softened	8 oz.	250 g
Curry powder	1/4 tsp.	1 mL
Salad dressing (or mayonnaise)	1 cup	250 mL
Finely chopped onion	1/2 cup	125 mL
Finely chopped celery	1/2 cup	125 mL
Can of corned beef (see Note, this page), mashed	6 1/2 oz.	184 g

Sprinkle gelatin over cold water in large saucepan. Let stand for 1 minute.

Add mushroom soup, cream cheese and curry powder. Heat and stir on medium until smooth. Chill until slightly thickened.

Add salad dressing, onion and celery. Fold in corned beef. Pour into 6 cup (1.5 L) mold. Chill for at least 1 hour to set. Just before serving, unmold onto serving plate. Makes about 5 cups (1.25 L).

2 tbsp. (30 mL): 82 Calories; 7.8 g Total Fat (3.5 g Mono, 1.9 g Poly, 2.2 g Sat); 14 mg Cholesterol; 1 g Carbohydrate; trace Fibre; 2 g Protein; 151 mg Sodium

Pictured on page 33.

Expect rave reviews when you serve this savoury spread.

note

An economical substitution for 2 cans of small shrimp is 1 1/2 cups (375 mL) frozen small shrimp, thawed.

Shrimp Spread

Salad dressing (or mayonnaise)	1/2 cup	125 mL
Butter (not margarine), softened	1/2 cup	125 mL
Cans of small shrimp (4 oz.,113 g, each), drained (see Note, this page)	2	2
Minced onion flakes	1 tbsp.	15 mL
Garlic powder	1/8 tsp.	0.5 mL
Lemon juice	1 tbsp.	15 mL

(continued on next page)

Cream salad dressing and butter in medium bowl.

Add shrimp, onion flakes, garlic powder and lemon juice. Mix. Spread in small serving dish. Makes about 2 cups (500 mL).

2 tbsp. (30 mL): 118 Calories; 11.7 g Total Fat (4.8 g Mono, 2.2 g Poly, 4.2 g Sat); 41 mg Cholesterol; trace Carbohydrate; trace Fibre; 3 g Protein; 116 mg Sodium

Pictured on page 33.

Toast Cups

White (or whole wheat) sandwich bread slices, crusts removed	9	9

Cut each bread slice into 4 squares or 2 1/2 inch (6.4 cm) circles. Press into ungreased muffin cups. Bake on bottom rack in 350°F (175°C) oven for about 15 minutes until browned. Cool. Makes 36 toast cups.

1 toast cup: 15 Calories; 0.2 g Total Fat (0.1 g Mono, trace Poly, 0.1 g Sat); trace Cholesterol; 3 g Carbohydrate; trace Fibre; trace Protein; 30 mg Sodium

Pictured on page 33 and on back cover.

TOAST POINTS

Arrange uncut bread slices on ungreased baking sheet. Broil, 1 side only, until lightly toasted. (Diagram #1) Cut each slice down the centre to make 2 rectangles. Cut each rectangle diagonally to make 4 elongated triangles.

Diagram 1

TOAST SQUARES

Arrange uncut bread slices on ungreased baking sheet. Broil, 1 side only, until lightly toasted. (Diagram #2) Cut each slice into 4 squares.

Diagram 2

TOAST TRIANGLES

Arrange uncut bread slices on ungreased baking sheet. Broil, 1 side only, until lightly toasted. (Diagram #3) Cut each slice diagonally from corner to corner into 4 even triangles.

Diagram 3

shrimp ball

Mix all 6 ingredients well. Shape into ball. Roll in 1/4 cup (60 mL) chopped fresh parsley and 2 tbsp. (30 mL) paprika.

Quick and easy "containers" for a dip, mousse or spread.

make ahead

Cool completely. Put into plastic bag or other airtight container. Do not freeze if buttered.

serving suggestion

Serve Toast Cups (or any of the variations) with Surprise Spread, page 6, Hot Crab Dip, page 16, Corned Beef Mousse, page 30, Shrimp Spread, page 30, Crab Mousse, page 32, Ham And Cheese Ball, page 34, or Antipasto, page 46.

Looks so fancy when shaped in a mold. Lightly spray mold with non-stick cooking spray to make it easier to remove mousse.

serving suggestion

Surround with assorted crackers and Toast Cups, page 31. Provide a cocktail spreader or small spoon.

presentation idea

To add great colour, lightly blanch fresh asparagus spears. Cut red and yellow peppers into slivers. Arrange asparagus and peppers, standing up, in a small cup and set in centre of unmolded mousse.

Crab Mousse

Envelope of unflavoured gelatin (equivalent to 1 tbsp., 15 mL)	1	1
Cold water	1/4 cup	60 mL
Can of condensed cream of mushroom soup	10 oz.	284 mL
Block of cream cheese, softened	8 oz.	250 g
Salad dressing (or mayonnaise)	2/3 cup	150 mL
Finely chopped celery	3/4 cup	175 mL
Can of crabmeat, drained and cartilage removed, flaked	4 oz.	113 g
Worcestershire sauce	1 1/2 tsp.	7 mL
Onion flakes	1 tsp.	5 mL

Sprinkle gelatin over cold water in large saucepan. Let stand for 1 minute.

Add mushroom soup, cream cheese and salad dressing. Heat and stir on medium until smooth. Remove from heat. Chill until slightly thickened.

Add remaining 4 ingredients. Stir well. Pour into lightly greased 4 cup (1 L) ring mold or fish mold. Chill for at least 1 hour to set. Just before serving, unmold onto serving plate. Makes about 3 1/2 cups (875 mL).

2 tbsp. (30 mL): 84 Calories; 8.1 g Total Fat (3.4 g Mono, 1.9 g Poly, 2.5 g Sat); 13 mg Cholesterol; 1 g Carbohydrate; trace Fibre; 2 g Protein; 170 mg Sodium

Pictured on page 33.

Top Left: Corned Beef Mousse, page 30
Top Right: Shrimp Spread, page 30
Bottom Left: Toast Cups, page 31
Bottom Right: Crab Mousse, above

You probably have all of the ingredients on hand for this delicious spread.

ham roll canapés

Shape into log (rather than ball), slightly smaller in diameter than your favourite round cracker. Chill for 2 hours. Just before serving, cut into 1/4 inch (6 mm) slices and place on crackers.

Pictured on this page.

ham and cheese spread

Use only 1 can of flaked ham, making it creamier and just right for spreading. Serve in a bowl.

Left: Ham And Cheese Ball, this page
Right: Ham Roll Canapés, above

Ham And Cheese Ball

Block of cream cheese, softened	8 oz.	250 g
Cans of flaked ham (6 1/2 oz., 184 g, each)	2	2
Dried chives	2 tsp.	10 mL
Lemon juice	2 tsp.	10 mL
Worcestershire sauce	1/2 tsp.	2 mL
Chopped fresh parsley	1 cup	250 mL

Put cream cheese and ham into small bowl. Beat or mash until well mixed.

Add chives, lemon juice and Worcestershire sauce. Shape into ball. If too soft to shape into ball, chill for at least 1 hour.

Roll ball in parsley until coated. Chill for at least 1 hour. Makes 1 ball, 2 1/2 cups (625 mL).

2 tbsp. (30 mL): 66 Calories; 5.5 g Total Fat (1.8 g Mono, 0.3 g Poly, 3.1 g Sat); 21 mg Cholesterol; 1 g Carbohydrate; trace Fibre; 4 g Protein; 223 mg Sodium

Pictured below.

Brie In Pastry

Frozen puff pastry patty shells (from 10 1/2 oz., 300 g, package of 6), thawed (see Note, this page)	2	2
Small Brie cheese round (with rind)	4 oz.	125 g
Large egg, fork-beaten	1	1
Medium red apples, cut into thin wedges	2	2

Roll 1 pastry shell out on lightly floured surface to 5 1/2 to 6 inch (14 to 15 cm) circle.

Place cheese round in middle of pastry. Bring up sides, pleating dough around edge. Roll out second pastry shell. Cut circle to fit top, using Brie tin. Crimp and seal edges. Make decorative shapes from scraps of pastry. Place on top.

Brush pastry with egg. Place on greased baking sheet. Bake in 450°F (230°C) oven for 15 minutes. Reduce heat to 350°F (175°C). Bake for about 5 minutes until golden brown. Transfer to serving plate.

Place apple wedges around pastry. Serves 6.

1 serving: 200 Calories; 13.1 g Total Fat (3.4 g Mono, 4 g Poly, 4.8 g Sat); 57 mg Cholesterol; 15 g Carbohydrate; 1 g Fibre; 7 g Protein; 183 mg Sodium

Pictured below.

Fruit and hot cheese make a great appetizer.

note

All 6 shells may be used to make 3 Brie pastries for a larger party. Simply triple the recipe.

make ahead

Assemble but don't brush with egg. Wrap and freeze. Thaw and bake as directed just before serving.

What an impressive appetizer—summer or winter!

notes

Use gloves when chopping hot peppers, as the caustic, oily compound called capsaicin (kap-SAY-ih-sihn) permeates the skin and causes an intense burning sensation.

If cilantro is not your favourite herb, double the amount of chopped parsley and omit the cilantro.

serving suggestion

Use Fruity Salsa as an accompaniment for chicken, fish or pork as well.

variation

If you don't have an electric grill or gas barbecue, toast baguette slices on both sides under broiler. Heat Brie cheese rounds in 325°F (160°C) oven for 5 to 10 minutes until softened.

Grilled Brie And Fruit Crostini

FRUITY SALSA

Diced mango	1/2 cup	125 mL
Diced red apple (with peel)	1/2 cup	125 mL
Canned white kidney beans, drained, rinsed and coarsely chopped	1/2 cup	125 mL
Finely chopped red onion	2 tbsp.	30 mL
Small hot pepper (your choice), seeded and finely diced (see Note, this page), optional	1	1
Balsamic vinegar	2 tbsp.	30 mL
Granulated sugar	1 tsp.	5 mL
Chopped fresh parsley	1 tbsp.	15 mL
Chopped fresh cilantro (see Note, this page)	1 tbsp.	15 mL
Baguette bread slices, cut 1/2 inch (12 mm) thick	24	24
Small Brie cheese rounds (with rind), 4 oz. (125 g) each	2	2
Olive (or cooking) oil	1/4 cup	60 mL

Fruity Salsa: Combine first 9 ingredients in small bowl. Cover. Let stand at room temperature for 1 hour, stirring several times, to blend flavours. Makes 2 cups (500 mL) salsa.

Preheat lightly greased electric grill to medium. Lightly brush baguette slices and cheese rounds with olive oil on both sides. Place baguette slices on grill. Cook for about 1 minute, turning to toast both sides. Increase heat to medium-high. Place cheese rounds on grill. Cook for 4 to 5 minutes on each side, turning carefully, until soft to touch. Arrange on serving platter with Fruity Salsa and baguette slices. Makes 24 servings.

1 serving: 92 Calories; 5.6 g Total Fat (2.7 g Mono, 0.4 g Poly, 2.2 g Sat); 10 mg Cholesterol; 7 g Carbohydrate; 1 g Fibre; 3 g Protein; 133 mg Sodium

Pictured on page 37.

An easy, one-step recipe using ingredients that you will probably have on hand. Serve warm.

dippers

Blisters, this page, Cheese Thins, page 39, corn chips

variation

Substitute a few finely chopped slices of jalapeño pepper for the hot pepper sauce. Then you really will have fire!

The best kind of blisters to have! People are intrigued by the name.

make ahead

Bake up to 3 days ahead. Cool completely. Store in airtight container or freeze for up to 6 months.

serving suggestion

Serve with Spreading Forest Fire, this page.

Spreading Forest Fire

Can of baked beans in tomato sauce, drained and mashed	14 oz.	398 mL
Grated sharp Cheddar cheese	1 cup	250 mL
Hard margarine (or butter)	1/2 cup	125 mL
Very finely chopped onion	1/2 cup	125 mL
Hot pepper sauce	1/2 tsp.	2 mL
Garlic powder	1/4 tsp.	1 mL
Salt	1/4 tsp.	1 mL
Pepper	1/8 tsp.	0.5 mL

Finely diced peppers (your choice), for garnish

Put first 8 ingredients into medium saucepan. Heat and stir until cheese and margarine are melted.

Transfer to serving bowl. Garnish with diced peppers. Makes 3 cups (750 mL).

2 tbsp. (30 mL): 71 Calories; 5.5 g Total Fat (3 g Mono, 0.5 g Poly, 1.8 g Sat); 5 mg Cholesterol; 4 g Carbohydrate; 1 g Fibre; 2 g Protein; 167 mg Sodium

Pictured on page 39.

Blisters

All-purpose flour	1 1/4 cups	300 mL
Salt	1/4 tsp.	1 mL
Hard margarine (or butter)	6 tbsp.	100 mL
Grated Havarti cheese	1 cup	250 mL
Cold water	1/3 cup	75 mL
Worcestershire sauce	1 tsp.	5 mL

Combine flour and salt in medium bowl. Cut in margarine until crumbly. Add cheese. Stir.

Combine cold water and Worcestershire sauce in small cup. Add to flour mixture. Stir until dough forms a ball. Divide dough into 8 portions. Roll each portion into paper-thin circle on lightly floured surface, turning over a few times to prevent sticking. Cut each circle into 8 wedges. Arrange in single layer on ungreased baking sheet. Bake on rack in top third of 350°F (175°C) oven for about 10 minutes until browned. Makes 64 wedges.

1 wedge: 25 Calories; 1.6 g Total Fat (0.8 g Mono, 0.1 g Poly, 0.5 g Sat); 2 mg Cholesterol; 2 g Carbohydrate; trace Fibre; 1 g Protein; 37 mg Sodium

Pictured on page 39.

Cheese Thins

All-purpose flour	2 cups	500 mL
Grated sharp Cheddar cheese	1 cup	250 mL
Granulated sugar	1 tbsp.	15 mL
Baking soda	1/2 tsp.	2 mL
Salt	1/2 tsp.	2 mL
Onion powder	1/4 tsp.	1 mL
Cayenne pepper	1/16 tsp.	0.5 mL
Water	1/2 cup	125 mL
Cooking oil	1/4 cup	60 mL

Put first 7 ingredients into medium bowl. Stir well.

Add water and cooking oil. Mix until dough forms a ball. Cover. Let stand for 20 minutes. Divide dough into 8 portions. Roll each portion into paper-thin circle on lightly floured surface. Cut each circle into 8 wedges. Arrange in single layer on ungreased baking sheet. Bake in 375°F (190°C) oven for about 10 minutes until crisp and browned. Makes 64 wedges.

1 wedge: 31 Calories; 1.6 g Total Fat (0.7 g Mono, 0.3 g Poly, 0.5 g Sat); 2 mg Cholesterol; 3 g Carbohydrate; trace Fibre; 1 g Protein; 40 mg Sodium

Pictured below.

These large, thin wafers are nice and crisp. Make a showy basketful.

serving suggestion

Serve with Dilly Dip, page 17, or Spreading Forest Fire, page 38.

Left: Cheese Thins, this page
Centre: Blisters, page 38
Right: Spreading Forest Fire, page 38

A hot and spicy dip with a definite mushroom and onion presence. This will be a huge hit at any gathering!

make ahead

Assemble but don't bake. Cover and chill for up to 2 days.

dippers

Assorted crackers, bread sticks, fresh vegetables (such as broccoli florets, carrot sticks, cherry or grape tomatoes, olives, pickled peppers, zucchini slices), pita wedges

variation

Serve cold if a thicker dip is desired.

Hot Mushroom Dip

Hard margarine (or butter)	2 tbsp.	30 mL
Finely chopped onion	1 cup	250 mL
Garlic clove, minced (or 1/4 tsp., 1 mL, powder), optional	1	1
Chopped fresh white mushrooms	3 cups	750 mL
Block of cream cheese, softened and cut into 8 pieces	8 oz.	250 g
Seasoned salt	1/2 tsp.	2 mL
Dill weed	1/2 tsp.	2 mL
Pepper, heavy sprinkle		
Grated Monterey Jack With Jalapeño cheese	1 1/2 cups	375 mL
Mayonnaise (not salad dressing)	1/2 cup	125 mL

Sliced fresh mushrooms, for garnish
Chopped chives, for garnish

Melt margarine in large frying pan on medium. Add onion, garlic and chopped mushrooms. Cook for about 10 minutes until liquid is evaporated and mushrooms are golden. Remove from heat.

Add next 4 ingredients. Stir until cream cheese is melted.

Add Monterey Jack cheese and mayonnaise. Mix well. Spread in ungreased 9 inch (22 cm) pie plate or shallow casserole. Bake in 350°F (175°C) oven for about 30 minutes until heated through.

Sprinkle with sliced mushrooms and chives. Makes 2 1/2 cups (625 mL).

2 tbsp. (30 mL): 131 Calories; 12.5 g Total Fat (5.2 g Mono, 1.9 g Poly, 4.9 g Sat); 24 mg Cholesterol; 2 g Carbohydrate; trace Fibre; 3 g Protein; 153 mg Sodium

Pictured on page 41.

Pronounced kon-KAY-soh. No need to go south of the border to enjoy this Mexican favourite.

dippers

Fresh vegetables, tortilla chips

Chili Con Queso

Can of stewed tomatoes (with juice), broken up	14 oz.	398 mL
Chopped onion	1 cup	250 mL
Garlic powder	1/4 tsp.	1 mL
Can of diced green chilies (with liquid)	4 oz.	113 g
Pasteurized cheese loaf (such as Velveeta), cut up	17 1/2 oz.	500 g

Put first 4 ingredients into medium saucepan. Stir. Cook, uncovered, on medium until liquid is evaporated.

Add cheese. Heat and stir on low until melted. Makes 4 cups (1 L).

2 tbsp. (30 mL): 51 Calories; 3.4 g Total Fat (1 g Mono, 0.1 g Poly, 2.1 g Sat); 9 mg Cholesterol; 2 g Carbohydrate; trace Fibre; 3 g Protein; 273 mg Sodium

Pictured above.

Chili Cheese Log

Grated medium Cheddar cheese	3 cups	750 mL
Block of cream cheese, softened	4 oz.	125 g
Worcestershire sauce	3/4 tsp.	4 mL
Garlic salt	1/2 tsp.	2 mL
Pepper	1/4 tsp.	1 mL
Chili powder	1/4 cup	60 mL

Put first 5 ingredients into medium bowl. Beat until smooth. Roll into 2 logs. Make diameter slightly smaller than your favourite cracker so slices will fit on top.

Spread chili powder on waxed paper or plate. Roll each log in chili powder until coated. Wrap in waxed paper or plastic wrap. Chill for 3 or 4 days to blend flavours. Cuts into 48 to 60 slices.

1 slice: 41 Calories; 3.5 g Total Fat (1 g Mono, 0.1 g Poly, 2.2 g Sat); 11 mg Cholesterol; 1 g Carbohydrate; trace Fibre; 2 g Protein; 74 mg Sodium

Pictured below.

An unusual, but delicious, appetizer that is easy to make and fun to serve.

make ahead

Prepare 3 or 4 days ahead to give flavours time to blend, or wrap tightly and freeze for up to 6 months.

serving suggestion

Place pre-cut slices on crackers or serve log with cheese knife and assorted crackers and let your guests help themselves.

Garnish with sour cream.

make ahead

Prepare day before. Store in refrigerator until ready to serve.

serving suggestion

Serve with assorted breads and crackers, or serve in wedges as a first course for a sit-down dinner.

Blue Cheesecake

Fine dry bread crumbs	2 tbsp.	30 mL
Grated Parmesan cheese	1 tbsp.	15 mL
Bacon slices, diced	8	8
Finely chopped onion	1 cup	250 mL
Blocks of cream cheese (8 oz., 250 g, each), softened	3	3
Blue cheese, crumbled	4 oz.	113 g
Large eggs	4	4
Sour cream	1/2 cup	125 mL
Hot pepper sauce	1/4 tsp.	1 mL

Combine bread crumbs and Parmesan cheese in small bowl. Grease bottom and side of 9 inch (22 cm) springform pan. Coat with crumb mixture, shaking off excess.

Cook bacon in frying pan on medium for 3 minutes. Add onion. Cook and stir until onion is soft and bacon is crisp. Drain.

Beat cream cheese, blue cheese and 1 egg in medium bowl until smooth. Little bits of blue cheese will remain. Add remaining eggs, 1 at a time, beating only until blended.

Add sour cream. Beat until well mixed. Add hot pepper sauce and bacon mixture. Stir. Pour into prepared pan. Bake in 325°F (160°C) oven for 1 to 1 1/2 hours until centre jiggles slightly when shaken. Immediately run sharp knife around top edge to allow cheesecake to settle evenly. Cool. Cover. Chill for 4 hours or overnight. Cuts into 20 thin wedges.

1 wedge: 197 Calories; 17.9 g Total Fat (5.4 g Mono, 0.9 g Poly, 10.6 g Sat); 93 mg Cholesterol; 3 g Carbohydrate; trace Fibre; 7 g Protein; 255 mg Sodium

Pictured on page 45.

Use some, freeze some—you'll always be prepared for unexpected entertaining. Make this traditional recipe with a friend. Share one batch or double the recipe and divide it.

note

Jar sizes of the sweet mixed pickles may vary. Buy whatever is closest to 12 oz. (341 mL).

serving suggestion

Serve with assorted crackers and Toast Cups, page 31, or spoon about 1 tsp. (5 mL) into croustades.

presentation idea

Antipasto makes the perfect gift for a dinner host, for new parents (for all those relatives and friends who drop by to take a peek at the new baby) or for a friend who did you a favour. Put a fancy lid on the jar, make a fabric topper, or simply tie a pretty ribbon around the lid. Attach a label that says "Can be stored in refrigerator for up to 1 week after thawing or opening."

Antipasto

Finely chopped cauliflower	1 cup	250 mL
Finely chopped pitted ripe olives	1/2 cup	125 mL
Chopped pickled onion	1/2 cup	125 mL
Finely chopped pimiento-stuffed olives	1/4 cup	60 mL
Cooking oil	1/4 cup	60 mL
Can of mushroom stems and pieces, drained and chopped	10 oz.	284 mL
Small green pepper, finely chopped	1	1
Ketchup	2 1/4 cups	550 mL
Jar of sweet mixed pickles, juice reserved, finely chopped (see Note, this page)	12 oz.	341 mL
Finely chopped red pepper (optional)	1/4 cup	60 mL
Reserved sweet pickle juice	3 tbsp.	50 mL
Can of flaked tuna, drained	6 1/2 oz.	184 g
Can of small shrimp, drained	4 oz.	113 g

Put first 5 ingredients into large saucepan. Cook, uncovered, on medium for 10 minutes, stirring occasionally.

Add next 6 ingredients. Bring to a boil. Reduce heat to medium-low. Simmer, uncovered, for 10 minutes, stirring often.

Add tuna and shrimp. Stir. Chill. Makes 6 cups (1.5 L).

2 tbsp. (30 mL): 39 Calories; 1.6 g Total Fat (0.9 g Mono, 0.4 g Poly, 0.2 g Sat); 5 mg Cholesterol; 5 g Carbohydrate; trace Fibre; 2 g Protein; 242 mg Sodium

Pictured on page 47 and on back cover.

Your guests will be impressed with this homemade, colourful salsa.

note

Use gloves when chopping hot peppers, as the caustic, oily compound called capsaicin (kap-SAY-ih-sihn) permeates the skin and causes an intense burning sensation.

time saver

Use your food processor to speed up preparation. If you prefer your salsa chunky, only process it for a few seconds.

make ahead

Cover and store in refrigerator for up to 1 week.

serving suggestion

Serve with an assortment of tortilla chips.

Quick Salsa

Small garlic clove	1	1
Jalapeño pepper, halved and seeded (see Note, this page)	1	1
Medium green or yellow pepper, cut into chunks	1/2	1/2
Medium red onion, cut into chunks	1/2	1/2
Medium roma (plum) tomatoes, quartered	6	6
Fresh cilantro, to taste (optional)		
Salt	1/2 tsp.	2 mL
Ground cumin	1/8 tsp.	0.5 mL
Pepper, sprinkle		
Can of diced green chilies, drained	4 oz.	113 g
Lime juice	2 tsp.	10 mL

Secure knife blade in food processor bowl. With motor running, drop garlic clove and jalapeño pepper through feed chute. Turn off.

Remove lid. Add green pepper and red onion to processor bowl. Secure lid. Pulse with on/off motion 8 to 10 times until coarsely diced. Scrape down processor bowl with spatula.

Add tomato, cilantro, salt, cumin and pepper. Secure lid. Pulse several times. Scrape sides down. Pulse several times until salsa is desired texture. Transfer to medium bowl.

Stir in green chilies and lime juice. Cover. Let stand at room temperature for 1 hour to blend flavours. Makes 3 1/2 cups (875 mL).

2 tbsp. (30 mL): 5 Calories; 0.1 g Total Fat (trace Mono, trace Poly, trace Sat); 0 mg Cholesterol; 1 g Carbohydrate; trace Fibre; trace Protein; 71 mg Sodium

Pictured on page 49.

Your guests will appreciate these colourful little alternatives to baguette slices or crackers.

serving suggestion

Accompany these with a soft cheese, such as Brie or Camembert, for easy spreading. Especially good with Layered Camembert, this page.

Welsh Cakes

All-purpose flour	2 cups	500 mL
Granulated sugar	1/2 cup	125 mL
Baking powder	2 tsp.	10 mL
Salt	1/2 tsp.	2 mL
Ground nutmeg	1/4 tsp.	1 mL
Ground cinnamon	1/4 tsp.	1 mL
Hard margarine (or butter)	1/2 cup	125 mL
Currants	1/2 cup	125 mL
Cut mixed peel, finely chopped	1/4 cup	60 mL
Large egg, fork-beaten	1	1
Milk	1/3 cup	75 mL

Combine first 6 ingredients in large bowl. Cut in margarine until crumbly.

Stir in currants and peel.

Add egg and milk. Stir until dough forms a ball. Roll on lightly floured surface to 1/4 inch (6 mm) thickness. Cut into 2 or 3 inch (5 or 7.5 cm) rounds. Heat frying pan on medium-low. Cook cakes, in batches, until both sides are browned. Pan should be lower temperature than for cooking pancakes. Serve cold. Makes 24 to 36 small cakes.

1 cake: 113 Calories; 4.4 g Total Fat (2.7 g Mono, 0.5 g Poly, 0.9 g Sat); 9 mg Cholesterol; 17 g Carbohydrate; 1 g Fibre; 2 g Protein; 132 mg Sodium

Pictured on page 51.

An excellent way to dress up this soft cheese. Very pretty for a wedding or baby shower.

serving suggestion

Serve with crackers or Welsh Cakes, this page. Provide a cocktail spreader.

Layered Camembert

Small Camembert cheese round	4 oz.	125 g
Block of cream cheese, softened	4 oz.	125 g
Orange juice	1 tbsp.	15 mL
Sliced almonds	2 tbsp.	30 mL
Seedless red grapes, sliced	2 tbsp.	30 mL

(continued on next page)

Cut cheese round in half horizontally.

Mash cream cheese in small bowl. Stir in orange juice.

Add almonds and grapes. Mix well. Spread all but 1 tbsp. (15 mL) cream cheese mixture over bottom layer of cheese round. Place top layer of cheese round over top. Spread remaining cream cheese mixture over top. Serves 8 to 10.

1 serving: 160 Calories; 13.9 g Total Fat (4.3 g Mono, 0.6 g Poly, 8.3 g Sat); 40 mg Cholesterol; 1 g Carbohydrate; trace Fibre; 8 g Protein; 309 mg Sodium

Pictured below.

presentation idea

Place in centre of serving plate. Arrange Welsh Cakes, page 50, on either side. Add clusters of seedless grapes for colour.

Left: Welsh Cakes, page 50
Right: Layered Camembert, page 50

This is so quick and so easy to make. Enjoy!

dippers

Assorted colours of tortilla chips, Tortilla Chips, page 10, Tortilla Crisps, page 10

Refried Bean Dip

Can of refried beans	14 oz.	398 mL
Salsa	2 tsp.	10 mL
Lean ground beef	1 lb.	454 g
Salsa	1/2 cup	125 mL
Salt, sprinkle		
Grated medium Cheddar cheese	1 cup	250 mL
Salsa	1/2 cup	125 mL
Non-fat sour cream	1 cup	250 mL
Finely chopped green onion	2 tbsp.	30 mL
Shredded iceberg lettuce	1 cup	250 mL
Medium tomato, seeded and chopped	1	1

Combine beans and first amount of salsa in small bowl. Spread evenly in ungreased 10 inch (25 cm) pie plate.

Scramble-fry ground beef in non-stick frying pan until no longer pink. Drain off fat.

Add second amount of salsa and salt to beef. Cook on medium for 5 minutes. Spread beef mixture evenly over bean mixture.

Sprinkle with cheese. Bake in 350°F (175°C) oven for about 15 minutes until cheese is melted and beans are hot. Cool for 10 minutes.

Spread with third amount of salsa.

Combine sour cream and green onion in separate small bowl. Spread over salsa.

Sprinkle with lettuce and tomato. Makes 4 cups (1 L).

2 tbsp. (30 mL): 56 Calories; 2.6 g Total Fat (0.9 g Mono, 0.1 g Poly, 1.3 g Sat); 11 mg Cholesterol; 4 g Carbohydrate; trace Fibre; 5 g Protein; 96 mg Sodium

Pictured on page 53.

Top Left: Refried Bean Dip, above
Bottom Right: Mexican Snackies, page 54

A colourful appetizer with an easy biscuit crust. Watch out for the nip in the taste!

make ahead

Prepare and bake biscuit crust ahead of time. Place in resealable freezer bag or wrap in plastic wrap. Chill for up to 24 hours or freeze for up to 2 months.

Mexican Snackies

Biscuit mix	2 cups	500 mL
Chopped fresh cilantro (or fresh parsley)	1/4 cup	60 mL
Water	1/2 cup	125 mL
Lean ground beef	1/2 lb.	225 g
Can of refried beans with green chilies	14 oz.	398 mL
Non-fat sour cream	1 cup	250 mL
Envelope of taco seasoning mix	1 1/4 oz.	35 g
Grated medium Cheddar cheese	1 1/2 cups	375 mL
Medium tomato, seeded and finely diced	1	1
Finely chopped green onion	1/2 cup	125 mL
Finely chopped green pepper	1/4 cup	60 mL
Finely chopped red pepper	1/4 cup	60 mL
Finely chopped pitted ripe whole olives	1/4 cup	60 mL

Combine biscuit mix and cilantro in medium bowl. Add water. Stir until soft dough forms. Turn out onto surface coated lightly with biscuit mix. Knead 10 times. Press in ungreased 10 x 15 inch (25 x 38 cm) jelly roll pan. Dough will be very thin. Bake in 400°F (205°C) oven for about 10 minutes until golden and firm. Cool.

Scramble-fry ground beef in non-stick frying pan until no longer pink. Drain.

Add refried beans. Mix. Cool slightly. Spread on crust.

Combine sour cream and seasoning mix in small bowl. Spread on beef mixture. Sprinkle with cheese.

Combine remaining 5 ingredients in separate medium bowl. Sprinkle over cheese. Pack down lightly. Chill for 1 hour. Cut into 1 1/2 x 2 inch (3.8 x 5 cm) pieces. Makes 40 appetizers.

1 appetizer: 79 Calories; 3.3 g Total Fat (1.2 g Mono, 0.4 g Poly, 1.4 g Sat); 8 mg Cholesterol; 9 g Carbohydrate; trace Fibre; 4 g Protein; 264 mg Sodium

Pictured on page 53.

Cheese Cubes

White sandwich bread loaf (unsliced)	1	1
Grated sharp Cheddar cheese	1 cup	250 mL
Hard margarine (or butter)	1/2 cup	125 mL
Block of cream cheese	4 oz.	125 g
Egg whites (large), room temperature	2	2

Cut crusts from bread loaf. Cut bread into 1 inch (2.5 cm) cubes. Put into resealable freezer bag. Put into freezer until ready to dip.

Put Cheddar cheese, margarine and cream cheese into top of double boiler. Heat over boiling water, stirring often, until melted. Remove from heat.

Beat egg whites in small bowl until stiff peaks form. Fold into cheese mixture. Dip bread cubes into cheese mixture with fork until all sides are coated. Use knife to help spread if needed. Arrange in single layer on ungreased baking sheet. Chill overnight. Just before serving, bake in 400°F (205°C) oven for about 10 minutes until golden brown. Makes about 60 cheese cubes.

1 cheese cube: 50 Calories; 3.3 g Total Fat (1.6 g Mono, 0.3 g Poly, 1.3 g Sat); 4 mg Cholesterol; 4 g Carbohydrate; trace Fibre; 1 g Protein; 80 mg Sodium

Pictured below.

You'll love these when they're hot and enjoy the leftovers cold—if there are any!

make ahead

Freeze, unbaked, on baking sheet until firm. Transfer frozen cubes to resealable freezer bag. Freeze for up to 2 months. Just before serving, thaw and bake as directed.

variation

Use Swiss cheese instead of Cheddar cheese for a lighter colour and a milder flavour.

These are a winner every time.

make ahead

Freeze baked tarts (in foil cups) in airtight container for up to 3 months. Just before serving, reheat thawed tarts in 325°F (160°C) oven for 15 to 20 minutes (or 30 to 40 minutes if still frozen) until heated through. Remove from foil cups.

Cheese Tarts

Milk	1/2 cup	125 mL
Large egg	1	1
Grated medium Cheddar cheese	1/2 cup	125 mL
Grated Havarti (or other white) cheese	1/2 cup	125 mL
Chopped onion	1 tbsp.	15 mL
Salt	1/4 tsp.	1 mL
Pepper, just a pinch		
Dry mustard, just a pinch		
Frozen mini-tart shells, thawed	24	24

Process first 8 ingredients in blender until smooth.

Place tart shells on ungreased baking sheet. Divide cheese mixture among tart shells. Bake in 350°F (175°C) oven for 20 to 25 minutes until set. Remove tarts from foil cups. Makes 24 tarts.

1 tart: 59 Calories; 4.1 g Total Fat (1.7 g Mono, 0.6 g Poly, 1.6 g Sat); 14 mg Cholesterol; 3 g Carbohydrate; trace Fibre; 2 g Protein; 111 mg Sodium

Pictured on page 57.

This combination of salmon and ham creates a tasty topping.

note

Red salmon is best for colour. If using red salmon, omit the paprika.

make ahead

Prepare and chill spread up to 2 days ahead or freeze for up to 3 months.

Salmon Canapés

Cans of salmon (7 1/2 oz., 213 g, each), drained and round bones removed, flaked (see Note, this page)	2	2
Block of cream cheese, softened	8 oz.	250 g
Can of flaked ham	6 1/2 oz.	184 g
Lemon juice	2 tsp.	10 mL
Prepared horseradish	1 tsp.	5 mL
Liquid smoke	1 tsp.	5 mL
Onion powder	1/4 tsp.	1 mL
Paprika (use with pink, not red, salmon)	2 tsp.	10 mL
Crackers (or small cocktail-size bread slices)	60	60

Chopped fresh parsley, for garnish

(continued on next page)

Put first 8 ingredients into medium bowl. Mix well. Makes 3 cups (750 mL) spread.

Spread about 2 tsp. (10 mL) salmon mixture on each cracker.

Sprinkle with parsley. Makes 60 canapés.

1 canapé: 43 Calories; 2.8 g Total Fat (1 g Mono, 0.4 g Poly, 1.2 g Sat); 9 mg Cholesterol; 2 g Carbohydrate; trace Fibre; 2 g Protein; 103 mg Sodium

Pictured below.

serving suggestion

As an alternative, serve salmon mixture in a bowl and crackers à la carte. Let everyone make their own canapés.

Left: Cheese Tarts, page 56
Centre Left: Salmon Canapés, page 56
Centre Right: Zippy Canapés, page 58
Right: Cheesy Meat Canapés, page 58

Visually impressive with red, green and white on dark bread.

make ahead

Freeze spread for up to 3 months.

presentation idea

To garnish, cut red and orange peppers into thin slices. Cut each slice on the diagonal to make small diamond shapes.

Keep these ingredients on hand for a quick and delicious last-minute appetizer.

make ahead

Prepare spread in morning and chill. Just before serving, assemble and bake as directed. Spread can also be frozen for up to 6 months if beef and sausage were not previously frozen.

Zippy Canapés

Block of light cream cheese, softened	8 oz.	250 g
Dried chives	2 tbsp.	30 mL
Seasoned salt	1/2 tsp.	2 mL
Finely chopped pimiento	1 tbsp.	15 mL
Small cocktail-size bread slices (such as pumpernickel)	48	48

Put cream cheese, chives and seasoned salt into small bowl. Mix well. Add pimiento. Stir. Makes 1 cup (250 mL) spread.

Spread or pipe about 1 tsp. (5 mL) cream cheese mixture on each bread slice. Makes 48 canapés.

1 canapé: 28 Calories; 1 g Total Fat (0.3 g Mono, 0.1 g Poly, 0.5 g Sat); 3 mg Cholesterol; 4 g Carbohydrate; trace Fibre; 1 g Protein; 104 mg Sodium

Pictured on page 57 and on back cover.

Cheesy Meat Canapés

Lean ground beef	1 lb.	454 g
Sausage meat	1 lb.	454 g
Pasteurized cheese loaf, cut up	17 1/2 oz.	500 g
Small cocktail-size bread slices (such as pumpernickel)	64	64

Scramble-fry ground beef and sausage meat in frying pan until no longer pink. Drain well.

Add cheese. Stir until melted. Makes 4 cups (1 L) spread.

Spread about 1 tbsp. (15 mL) meat mixture on each bread slice. Place on ungreased baking sheets. Bake in 350°F (175°C) oven for about 15 minutes until hot. Makes 64 canapés.

1 canapé: 71 Calories; 4.3 g Total Fat (1.5 g Mono, 0.3 g Poly, 2.1 g Sat); 13 mg Cholesterol; 4 g Carbohydrate; trace Fibre; 4 g Protein; 185 mg Sodium

Pictured on page 57.

Devilled Eggs

Large hard-boiled eggs (see Notes, this page)	6	6
Salad dressing (or mayonnaise)	2 tbsp.	30 mL
Sweet pickle relish	2 tbsp.	30 mL
Onion powder	1/4 – 1/2 tsp.	1 – 2 mL

Paprika, sprinkle

Cut eggs in half lengthwise. Remove yolks to small bowl. Place egg white halves on large plate.

Add salad dressing, relish and onion powder to egg yolks. Mash well with fork. Spoon or pipe into egg white halves.

Sprinkle with paprika. Makes 12 devilled eggs.

1 devilled egg: 54 Calories; 3.9 g Total Fat (1.7 g Mono, 0.8 g Poly, 0.9 g Sat); 108 mg Cholesterol; 2 g Carbohydrate; 0 g Fibre; 3 g Protein; 67 mg Sodium

Pictured below.

These are an all-season favourite.

notes

To make perfect hard-boiled eggs, poke wider end of each egg with an egg piercer. Put eggs into cold water in saucepan large enough to hold in single layer. Bring water to a boil on medium-high. Reduce heat to medium. Boil for exactly 10 minutes. Cool eggs under cold, running water until no heat can be felt when egg is held for 10 seconds. Refrigerate immediately (with or without shells).

When slicing hard-boiled eggs, wet knife first to keep yolk from crumbling, or purchase an egg slicer that has thin wire cutters.

This won't last long! Be prepared to refill the bowl several times. Also good for bag lunches and birthday parties.

make ahead

Cool completely. Freeze in airtight container for up to 6 months.

variation

Add 2 cups (500 mL) peanuts to popped corn before adding syrup mixture.

special caramel corn

Add 2 cups (500 mL) peanuts to the popped corn but make 1 1/2 times the syrup. Makes about 26 1/2 cups (6.6 L).

Pictured on this page.

Caramel Popcorn

Popped corn (about 1 cup, 250 mL, unpopped)	24 – 28 cups	6 – 7 L
Hard margarine (or butter)	1 cup	250 mL
Brown sugar, packed	2 cups	500 mL
Corn syrup	1/2 cup	125 mL
Salt	1 tsp.	5 mL
Vanilla	1 tsp.	5 mL
Baking soda	1/2 tsp.	2 mL

Put popped corn into extra-large bowl.

Combine margarine, brown sugar, corn syrup and salt in large heavy saucepan. Heat and stir on medium until boiling. Boil, without stirring, for 5 minutes.

Add vanilla and baking soda. Stir. Mixture will bubble and foam. Pour over popped corn. Toss until all pieces are coated. Spread on 2 large ungreased baking sheets. Bake in 250°F (120°C) oven for 1 hour, stirring every 15 minutes. Cool completely. Break apart. Store in resealable freezer bags. Makes about 24 cups (6 L).

1 cup (250 mL): 199 Calories; 8.4 g Total Fat (5.3 g Mono, 1 g Poly, 1.7 g Sat); 0 mg Cholesterol; 31 g Carbohydrate; 0 g Fibre; 1 g Protein; 237 mg Sodium

Pictured below.

Top Left: Caramel Popcorn, this page
Bottom Right: Special Caramel Corn, above

Snackin' Potato Skins

Medium baking potatoes, baked and cooled	5	5
Hard margarine (or butter), melted	1/4 cup	60 mL
Seasoned salt, sprinkle		

Cut potatoes in half lengthwise. Cut each half in half lengthwise. Cut all 20 strips in half crosswise, for a total of 40 pieces. Scoop away most of potato, leaving thin layer on each skin.

Brush both sides with margarine. Sprinkle with seasoned salt. Place, skin-side up, on ungreased baking sheet. Bake in 400°F (205°C) oven for 10 to 15 minutes until crisp. Makes 40 appetizers.

1 appetizer: 24 Calories; 1.1 g Total Fat (0.7 g Mono, 0.1 g Poly, 0.2 g Sat); 0 mg Cholesterol; 3 g Carbohydrate; trace Fibre; trace Protein; 15 mg Sodium

Pictured below.

These crisp, seasoned potato skins are always a hit.

serving suggestion

Serve with sour cream and chopped green onion on the side.

variations

Omit seasoned salt. Sprinkle with 1/2 envelope of taco seasoning mix. Bake as directed.

Omit margarine and seasoned salt. Place potato wedges, skin-side down, on ungreased baking sheet. Sprinkle with 1 cup (250 mL) grated Cheddar cheese. Add either 1/3 cup (75 mL) cooked and crumbled bacon, 1/3 cup (75 mL) chopped green onion, or a combination of both. Bake as directed.

Pronounced dohl-MAH-dehs, these are an eastern European delicacy.

Dolmades

Olive (or cooking) oil	2 tbsp.	30 mL
Finely chopped onion	1 1/2 cups	375 mL
Chopped pine nuts (or pecans)	1/2 cup	125 mL
Water	2 cups	500 mL
Basmati (or long grain white) rice	1 cup	250 mL
Dark raisins	2/3 cup	150 mL
Parsley flakes (or 1/4 cup, 60 mL, chopped fresh parsley)	1 tbsp.	15 mL
Medium tomato, seeded and chopped	1	1
Salt	1 tsp.	5 mL
Pepper	1/8 tsp.	0.5 mL
Ground cinnamon	1/4 tsp.	1 mL
Jar of grapevine leaves, drained (see Note, this page)	17 oz.	473 mL
Lemon juice	1 1/2 tbsp.	25 mL
Olive (or cooking) oil	2 tbsp.	30 mL
Water	1 cup	250 mL

Heat first amount of olive oil in frying pan on medium. Add onion. Cook for 5 to 10 minutes until soft.

Add pine nuts. Cook for about 5 minutes until browned.

Add first amount of water, rice, raisins and parsley. Stir. Bring to a gentle boil on medium. Reduce heat to medium-low. Cover. Simmer for 15 to 20 minutes until rice is tender and liquid is absorbed.

Add tomato, salt, pepper and cinnamon. Stir. Cool enough to handle.

Rinse grapevine leaves under warm water. Blot dry. Place 2 1/2 tbsp. (37 mL) rice mixture on each of 32 grapevine leaves. Roll stem end over rice, tucking in sides as you roll up. Cover bottom and sides of greased 2 quart (2 L) casserole with some remaining grapevine leaves. Arrange rolls, seam-side down, close together over leaves.

Sprinkle with lemon juice and second amount of olive oil. Cover surface with any remaining grapevine leaves. Add second amount of water. Cover. Bake in 350°F (175°C) oven for 1 hour. Cool. Makes 32 dolmades.

1 dolmade: 69 Calories; 3.2 g Total Fat (1.8 g Mono, 0.7 g Poly, 0.5 g Sat); 0 mg Cholesterol; 10 g Carbohydrate; 1 g Fibre; 2 g Protein; 186 mg Sodium

Pictured on this page.

Scallops With Bacon

Bacon slices, cut in half crosswise	6	6
Frozen sea (large) scallops	12	12
Boiling water, to cover		

Cook bacon in frying pan on medium until partially cooked. Do not cook too much or bacon will not be soft enough to roll when cooled. Remove to paper towels to drain. Cool.

Cook scallops in boiling water in medium saucepan for about 5 minutes until opaque. Drain. Cool. Roll 1 bacon piece around each scallop. Secure with wooden picks. Arrange in single layer on ungreased baking sheet. Bake in 425°F (220°C) oven for about 10 minutes until bacon is sizzling and scallops are heated through. Makes 12 appetizers.

1 appetizer: 24 Calories; 1.6 g Total Fat (0.8 g Mono, 0.2 g Poly, 0.6 g Sat); 5 mg Cholesterol; trace Carbohydrate; 0 g Fibre; 2 g Protein; 60 mg Sodium

Pictured above.

This gourmet treat uses only two ingredients! It's so easy to make and it will disappear in no time.

time saver

To save some preparation and cleanup time, wrap uncooked bacon around cooked scallops. Broil for about 5 minutes per side until bacon is crisp.

variation

If you feel daring, marinate the thawed, uncooked scallops in hot chili sauce for up to 1 hour.

A great combination of flavours works its magic on these jumbo shrimp.

variation

Shrimp can also be grilled on an electric grill or gas barbecue. Preheat electric grill for 5 minutes or barbecue to medium. Cook shrimp on greased grill for about 2 minutes per side, brushing several times with boiled marinade, until pink. Do not overcook.

Chili Lemon Shrimp

Olive (or cooking) oil	2 tbsp.	30 mL
Liquid honey	3 tbsp.	50 mL
Sweet (or regular) chili sauce	1/4 cup	60 mL
Finely grated lemon zest	1 tsp.	5 mL
Lemon juice	1/4 cup	60 mL
Chopped fresh parsley (or 1 1/2 tbsp., 25 mL, flakes)	2/3 cup	150 mL
Shallots (or green onions), finely chopped	2	2
Seasoned salt	1 tsp.	5 mL
Dried crushed chilies	2 tsp.	10 mL
Dry white (or alcohol-free) wine	2/3 cup	150 mL
Raw jumbo shrimp (about 25 to 30 with tails intact), peeled and deveined	2 1/4 lbs.	1 kg
Bamboo skewers (4 inch, 10 cm, length), soaked in water for 10 minutes	25 – 30	25 – 30

Combine first 10 ingredients in large bowl.

Add shrimp. Stir until coated. Cover. Marinate in refrigerator for 3 hours, turning several times. Remove shrimp. Pour marinade into small saucepan. Bring to a boil. Boil for 5 minutes.

Thread 1 shrimp, starting at head end, lengthwise onto each skewer. Place on ungreased baking sheet. Broil on top rack for about 2 minutes per side, basting with marinade several times, until shrimp are pink. Makes 25 to 30 shrimp.

1 shrimp: 72 Calories; 1.9 g Total Fat (0.9 g Mono, 0.4 g Poly, 0.3 g Sat); 61 mg Cholesterol; 4 g Carbohydrate; trace Fibre; 8 g Protein; 150 mg Sodium

Pictured on page 65 and on front cover.

One of the tastiest appetizers ever! Absolutely delectable.

note

Two 10 oz. (284 mL) cans of sliced mushrooms, drained and chopped, can be used in place of the fresh mushrooms.

make ahead

To freeze unbaked, do not brush with egg. Freeze on baking sheet until firm. Transfer frozen turnovers to resealable freezer bag. Freeze for up to 6 months. Just before serving, arrange frozen turnovers in single layer on greased baking sheet. Brush with egg. Bake in 350°F (175°C) oven for 20 to 30 minutes until heated through and browned. If already baked, heat frozen turnovers in 325°F (160°C) oven for 15 to 20 minutes until hot.

mushroom cups

Fill Toast Cups, page 31, with Mushroom Filling, this page. Heat in 400°F (205°C) oven for about 10 minutes until bubbly.

Mushroom Turnovers

CREAM CHEESE PASTRY

Block of cream cheese, softened	8 oz.	250 g
Hard margarine (or butter), softened	1/2 cup	125 mL
All-purpose flour	1 1/2 cups	375 mL

MUSHROOM FILLING

Hard margarine (or butter)	3 tbsp.	50 mL
Large onion, finely chopped	1	1
Fresh white mushrooms, chopped (see Note, this page)	1/2 lb.	225 g
All-purpose flour	2 tbsp.	30 mL
Salt	1 tsp.	5 mL
Pepper	1/4 tsp.	1 mL
Dried thyme	1/4 tsp.	1 mL
Sour cream	1/4 cup	60 mL
Large egg, fork-beaten	1	1

Cream Cheese Pastry: Beat cream cheese and margarine in medium bowl until well mixed. Add flour. Mix well. Shape into ball. Chill for at least 1 hour.

Mushroom Filling: Melt margarine in frying pan on medium. Add onion and mushrooms. Cook for about 10 minutes, stirring often, until softened.

Add flour, salt, pepper and thyme. Stir. Add sour cream. Heat and stir until thickened. Remove from heat. Cool.

Roll out pastry on lightly floured surface to 1/8 inch (3 mm) thickness. Cut into 3 inch (7.5 cm) circles. Place 1 tsp. (5 mL) filling in centre of each circle. Dampen half of outer edge with egg. Fold over. Press edges together with fork or fingers to seal. Arrange in single layer on greased baking sheets. Cut tiny slits in top of each turnover. Brush tops with egg. Bake in 450°F (230°C) oven for about 10 minutes until golden brown. Makes 36 to 48 turnovers.

1 turnover: 86 Calories; 6.5 g Total Fat (3.2 g Mono, 0.5 g Poly, 2.5 g Sat); 14 mg Cholesterol; 6 g Carbohydrate; trace Fibre; 2 g Protein; 132 mg Sodium

Pictured on page 67 and on back cover.

Tender, flaky phyllo pastry makes this delicious finger food even more tempting.

notes

There are two very different black bean sauce products available with the same name. What we refer to here is a thinner, smoother product that can be used as is. The concentrated version is paste-like and somewhat chunky. Both are found in the Asian section of the grocery store.

To toast sesame seeds, spread evenly in ungreased shallow pan. Bake in 350°F (175°C) oven for 5 to 10 minutes, stirring or shaking often, until desired doneness.

make ahead

Assemble in morning and keep well-covered with damp tea towel until just before baking. Bake as directed.

Beef Sprout Rolls

Cooking oil	1 tbsp.	15 mL
Finely chopped onion	1/2 cup	125 mL
Finely chopped celery	1/2 cup	125 mL
Coarsely chopped fresh bean sprouts	1 1/2 cups	375 mL
Grated carrot	1/2 cup	125 mL
Lean ground beef	1/2 lb.	225 g
Garlic clove, minced (or 1/4 tsp., 1 mL, powder)	1	1
Prepared black bean sauce (see Note, this page)	2 tbsp.	30 mL
Large eggs, fork-beaten	2	2
Salt	1/8 tsp.	0.5 mL
Coarsely ground pepper	1/8 tsp.	0.5 mL
Phyllo pastry sheets	8	8
Hard margarine (or butter), melted	2 tbsp.	30 mL
Sesame seeds, toasted (see Note, this page)	1 tbsp.	15 mL

Heat frying pan on medium-high. Add cooking oil. Add onion, celery, bean sprouts and carrot. Stir-fry for 5 minutes. Transfer to medium bowl.

Scramble-fry ground beef and garlic in same frying pan until beef is no longer pink. Drain off fat.

Add vegetables to beef. Mix well. Add black bean sauce. Stir-fry for 2 minutes.

Reduce heat to medium-low. Add eggs, salt and pepper. Heat and stir until eggs just start to set. Cool. Mixture should be moist.

Layer 2 sheets of phyllo pastry together, spraying each with cooking spray. Cut in half lengthwise. Cut each half crosswise into 2 pieces. Repeat with remaining pastry sheets, for a total of 32 pieces, keeping pastry covered with damp tea towel to prevent drying out.

(continued on next page)

Place 2 tsp. (10 mL) beef mixture along 1 long side of each pastry piece. Roll up, tucking in ends. Roll will be thin. Brush with margarine. Sprinkle with sesame seeds. Place rolls on greased baking sheets. Bake in 375°F (190°C) oven for about 13 minutes until golden. Makes 32 rolls.

1 roll: 47 Calories; 2.6 g Total Fat (1.3 g Mono, 0.5 g Poly, 0.6 g Sat); 17 mg Cholesterol; 4 g Carbohydrate; trace Fibre; 2 g Protein; 90 mg Sodium

Pictured below.

Left: Beef Sprout Rolls, page 68
Right: Tortilla Roll-Ups, page 70

These have become a favourite potluck appetizer. They're easy to make and the flavours of beef and pickle combine so well.

make ahead

Make the rolls the day before. Do not cut. Wrap tightly and chill. Just before serving, slice and secure with wooden picks.

time saver

To save last-minute kitchen work, make rolls in the morning. Wrap and chill for 1 hour. Slice and secure with wooden picks. Arrange in single layer on serving platter. Cover and chill until ready to serve. Keep remaining slices chilled in a covered container, ready to refill platter as necessary.

serving suggestion

Serve slightly chilled or at room temperature.

Tortilla Roll-Ups

Block of light cream cheese, softened	4 oz.	125 g
Low-fat salad dressing (or mayonnaise)	2 tbsp.	30 mL
Dijon mustard	2 tsp.	10 mL
Finely chopped dill pickles, blotted dry	1/4 cup	60 mL
Flour tortillas (10 inch, 25 cm, diameter)	3	3
Shaved deli roast beef	8 oz.	225 g

Combine cream cheese, salad dressing and mustard in small bowl until smooth. Add pickles. Mix well.

Divide and spread cream cheese mixture on each tortilla. Divide and layer beef on top. Roll up each tortilla very tightly. Wrap in plastic wrap. Chill for at least 1 hour. To serve, slice chilled rolls into 1 inch (2.5 cm) pieces. Secure with wooden picks. Makes 27 roll-ups.

1 roll-up: 46 Calories; 1.2 g Total Fat (0.7 g Mono, 0.2 g Poly, 0.7 g Sat); 9 mg Cholesterol; 3 g Carbohydrate; trace Fibre; 4 g Protein; 89 mg Sodium

Pictured on page 69.

Crunchies

All-purpose flour	1 1/2 cups	375 mL
Grated sharp Cheddar cheese	1 1/2 cups	375 mL
Hard margarine (or butter), softened	2/3 cup	150 mL
Baking powder	1 tsp.	5 mL
Salt	1/2 tsp.	2 mL
Cayenne pepper	1/4 tsp.	1 mL
Crisp rice cereal	1 cup	250 mL

These delightful little morsels have the melt-in-your-mouth texture of shortbread and the crunch of a crisp rice cereal.

Put first 6 ingredients into medium bowl. Mix well.

Add cereal. Mix with hands. Shape into 1 inch (2.5 cm) balls. Arrange in single layer on ungreased baking sheet. Bake in 375°F (190°C) oven for about 20 minutes until lightly browned. Makes 42 appetizers.

1 appetizer: 64 Calories; 4.5 g Total Fat (2.4 g Mono, 0.4 g Poly, 1.5 g Sat); 4 mg Cholesterol; 4 g Carbohydrate; trace Fibre; 2 g Protein; 107 mg Sodium

Pictured below.

The delicious sauce coats each meatball generously.

meatball tips

To make uniform meatballs:

1. Pat meat mixture into 1 inch (2.5 cm) thick square on waxed paper. Cut into 1 inch (2.5 cm) cubes. Dip hands into water and gently roll cubes into balls.

2. Roll meat mixture into log. Cut into 2 inch (5 cm) sections. Roll each section into ball.

3. Use smallest size ice-cream scoop to measure equal amounts of meat mixture for appetizer meatballs. The scoops are generally available through restaurant supply outlets or kitchen specialty shops.

make ahead

Arrange cooked meatballs in single layer on baking sheet. Freeze until firm. Transfer frozen meatballs to resealable freezer bag. Freeze for up to 3 months. Just before serving, reheat frozen meatballs on greased baking sheet with sides or in greased casserole in 350°F (175°C) oven for 15 to 20 minutes until heated through.

Maple-Glazed Meatballs

MEATBALLS		
Lean ground beef	1 1/2 lbs.	680 g
Prepared horseradish	2 tbsp.	30 mL
Dry bread crumbs	1 1/4 cups	300 mL
Large eggs, fork-beaten	2	2
Skim evaporated milk	1/2 cup	125 mL
MAPLE SAUCE		
Chili sauce	1/2 cup	125 mL
Corn (or cane) syrup	1/2 cup	125 mL
Soy sauce	2 tbsp.	30 mL
Dry mustard	1/2 tsp.	2 mL
Ground allspice	1/2 tsp.	2 mL
Cornstarch	2 tsp.	10 mL
Maple flavouring	1 1/2 tsp.	7 mL

Meatballs: Put all 5 ingredients into medium bowl. Mix well. Shape into 3/4 inch (2 cm) balls. (See Meatball Tips, this page.) Arrange in single layer on greased baking sheet. Bake in 450°F (230°C) oven for about 10 minutes until browned and no longer pink inside.

Maple Sauce: Combine all 7 ingredients in medium saucepan. Bring to a boil on medium, stirring often. Makes 1 1/4 cups (300 mL) sauce. Add meatballs. Stir until heated through. Makes about 96 meatballs.

1 meatball (with sauce): 31 Calories; 1.3 g Total Fat (0.5 g Mono, 0.1 g Poly, 0.5 g Sat); 9 mg Cholesterol; 3 g Carbohydrate; trace Fibre; 2 g Protein; 65 mg Sodium

Pictured on page 73.

Top Left: Maple-Glazed Meatballs, above
Bottom Right: Spanish Meatballs, page 74

Delightful meatballs with a savoury hint of wine and cloves.

make ahead

Arrange partially cooked meatballs in single layer on baking sheet. Freeze until firm. Transfer frozen meatballs to resealable freezer bag. Freeze for up to 3 months. Just before serving, add thawed meatballs to sauce. Finish cooking as directed in recipe.

Spanish Meatballs

MEATBALLS

Lean ground beef	1 lb.	454 g
Fresh whole wheat bread crumbs	1 cup	250 mL
Large egg, fork-beaten	1	1
Milk	2 tbsp.	30 mL
Garlic clove, minced (or 1/4 tsp., 1 mL, powder)	1	1
Salt	1/4 tsp.	1 mL
Pepper	1/4 tsp.	1 mL

SPANISH SAUCE

Olive (or cooking) oil	1 tbsp.	15 mL
Medium onion, finely chopped	1	1
Garlic cloves, minced (or 1/2 tsp., 2 mL, powder)	2	2
Beef bouillon powder	1/2 tsp.	2 mL
Boiling water	1/2 cup	125 mL
Tomato paste	1 tbsp.	15 mL
Dry white (or alcohol-free) wine	1/2 cup	125 mL
Cornstarch	2 tsp.	10 mL
Brown sugar, packed	1 tsp.	5 mL
Pepper	1/4 tsp.	1 mL
Ground cloves	1/8 tsp.	0.5 mL

Meatballs: Put all 7 ingredients into large bowl. Mix well. Shape into 1 inch (2.5 cm) balls. (See Meatball Tips, page 72.) Arrange in single layer on greased baking sheet. Bake in 350°F (175°C) oven for 10 minutes until browned. Meatballs may not be fully cooked. Drain. Set aside.

Spanish Sauce: Heat olive oil in medium saucepan on medium. Add onion and garlic. Cook for 2 to 3 minutes until onion is softened.

Dissolve bouillon powder in boiling water in small cup. Add to onion mixture. Stir. Add tomato paste. Stir.

Stir wine into cornstarch in same small cup until smooth. Gradually stir into tomato paste mixture. Heat and stir until boiling and thickened.

(continued on next page)

Add brown sugar, pepper and cloves. Stir. Makes about 1 1/4 cups (300 mL) sauce. Add meatballs. Heat on low for 25 to 30 minutes until meatballs are heated through and no longer pink inside. Makes about 36 meatballs.

1 meatball (with sauce): 34 Calories; 1.6 g Total Fat (0.8 g Mono, 0.1 g Poly, 0.5 g Sat); 13 mg Cholesterol; 1 g Carbohydrate; trace Fibre; 3 g Protein; 42 mg Sodium

Pictured on page 73.

Wiener Bites

| Bacon slices | 12 | 12 |
| Wieners, cut into 6 pieces each | 8 | 8 |

Cook bacon in frying pan on medium until partially cooked. Do not cook too much or bacon will not be soft enough to roll when cooled. When cool enough to handle, cut each slice in half crosswise and then lengthwise. Wrap each bacon piece around each wiener piece. Secure with wooden picks. Arrange in single layer on ungreased baking sheet. Bake in 400°F (205°C) oven for about 5 minutes until sizzling hot and bacon is cooked. Makes 48 appetizers.

1 appetizer: 32 Calories; 2.6 g Total Fat (1.3 g Mono, 0.3 g Poly, 1 g Sat); 5 mg Cholesterol; trace Carbohydrate; 0 g Fibre; 1 g Protein; 100 mg Sodium

Pictured below.

These are among the best. You'll have to make them in multiple quantities to keep the gang happy.

make ahead

Bake, drain and cool. Arrange in single layer on baking sheet. Freeze until firm. Transfer to resealable freezer bag. Reheat desired quantity as needed in 325°F (160°C) oven for 10 to 15 minutes until hot.

These lip-smacking wings have a delicious sweet and sour coating.

chicken wing tips

To cut whole wings, cut off tips of each wing with sharp knife. Spread wing apart at joint until it separates somewhat. Cut apart at separation.

Freeze discarded wing tips to use in making chicken broth at a later date. Raw tips can be frozen for up to 9 months.

make ahead

Arrange partially cooked drumettes in single layer on baking sheet. Freeze until firm. Transfer frozen drumettes to resealable freezer bag. Freeze for up to 1 month. Just before serving, arrange thawed drumettes in single layer on greased, foil-lined baking sheet with sides. Finish baking with sauce as directed in recipe.

Bali Wings

Chicken drumettes (or whole chicken wings, split in half and tips discarded; see Chicken Wing Tips, this page)	4 lbs.	1.8 kg
BALI SAUCE		
Brown sugar, packed	1/2 cup	125 mL
Granulated sugar	1/4 cup	60 mL
Cornstarch	1/4 cup	60 mL
Ground ginger	1/2 tsp.	2 mL
Salt	1/2 tsp.	2 mL
Pepper	1/4 tsp.	1 mL
Water	1 cup	250 mL
White vinegar	1/2 cup	125 mL
Soy sauce	1/3 cup	75 mL

Arrange drumettes in single layer on greased foil-lined baking sheet with sides. Bake in 350°F (175°C) oven for 30 minutes.

Bali Sauce: Put first 6 ingredients into small saucepan. Stir well.

Add water, vinegar and soy sauce. Heat and stir on medium until boiling and thickened. Brush sauce over drumettes. Bake for 15 to 20 minutes, turning and brushing with sauce at least 2 more times, until tender and no longer pink inside. Makes about 32 drumettes or 48 wing pieces.

1 drumette: 81 Calories; 3.9 g Total Fat (1.6 g Mono, 0.8 g Poly, 1.1 g Sat); 19 mg Cholesterol; 7 g Carbohydrate; trace Fibre; 5 g Protein; 237 mg Sodium

Pictured on page 78.

Buffalo Wings

Large eggs, fork-beaten	2	2
Milk	1/4 cup	60 mL
Hot pepper sauce	1 tbsp.	15 mL
All-purpose flour	2/3 cup	150 mL
Seasoned salt	2 tsp.	10 mL
Pepper	1/2 tsp.	2 mL
Chicken drumettes (or whole chicken wings, split in half and tips discarded; see Chicken Wing Tips, page 76)	3 lbs.	1.4 kg
Cooking oil, for deep-frying		
Commercial Louisiana hot sauce (see Note, this page)	1 – 4 tbsp.	15 – 60 mL

Combine eggs, milk and hot pepper sauce in small bowl.

Combine flour, seasoned salt and pepper in separate small bowl.

Dip each drumette into egg mixture. Dip into flour mixture until coated. Deep-fry, in batches, in hot (375°F, 190°C) cooking oil for 8 to 10 minutes until browned and crisp and no longer pink inside. Drain on paper towels. Put drumettes into large pail or bowl with cover.

Drizzle drumettes with hot sauce. Cover. Toss for 1 to 2 minutes until sauce is distributed evenly. Makes about 24 drumettes or 36 wing pieces.

1 drumette: 96 Calories; 6.7 g Total Fat (3.1 g Mono, 1.6 g Poly, 1.4 g Sat); 37 mg Cholesterol; 3 g Carbohydrate; trace Fibre; 6 g Protein; 143 mg Sodium

Pictured on page 78/79.

A mouth-watering addition to any casual gathering.

note

Decide if you want hot wings or "suicide" hot wings by varying the amount of Louisiana hot sauce.

make ahead

Arrange cooked drumettes in single layer on baking sheet. Freeze until firm. Transfer frozen drumettes to resealable freezer bag. Freeze for up to 1 month. Just before serving, reheat frozen drumettes on greased baking sheet with sides or in greased casserole in 350°F (175°C) oven for 15 to 20 minutes until heated through. Coat with sauce as directed in recipe.

serving suggestion

For a quick dipping sauce, use preferred quantity of blue cheese creamy salad dressing.

Pictured on Next Page:
Top Left: Crusty Parmesan Wings, page 80
Top Right: Sweet And Sour Wings, page 81
Centre Left: Bali Wings, page 76
Centre Right: Buffalo Wings, this page
Bottom: Parmesan Chicken Wings, page 80

Flavourful Parmesan cheese gives these wings a real lift.

make ahead

Arrange cooked drumettes in single layer on baking sheet. Freeze until firm. Transfer frozen drumettes to resealable freezer bag. Freeze for up to 1 month. Just before serving, reheat frozen drumettes on greased baking sheet with sides or in greased casserole in 350°F (175°C) oven for 15 to 20 minutes until heated through.

Crusty Parmesan Wings

Golden Italian salad dressing	3/4 cup	175 mL
Grated Parmesan cheese	1 cup	250 mL
Fine dry bread crumbs	1/2 cup	125 mL
Paprika	1 1/2 tsp.	7 mL
Chicken drumettes (or whole chicken wings, split in half and tips discarded; see Chicken Wing Tips, page 76)	3 lbs.	1.4 kg

Measure salad dressing into small bowl.

Put next 3 ingredients into separate small bowl. Mix well.

Dip each drumette into salad dressing. Dip into cheese mixture until coated. Arrange in single layer on greased foil-lined baking sheet with sides. Bake in 350°F (175°C) oven for about 45 minutes until tender and no longer pink inside. Makes about 24 drumettes or 36 wing pieces.

1 drumette: 133 Calories; 10.8 g Total Fat (5 g Mono, 2.7 g Poly, 2.4 g Sat); 28 mg Cholesterol; 2 g Carbohydrate; trace Fibre; 7 g Protein; 243 mg Sodium

Pictured on page 78.

These wings will get the conversation going. Better make lots.

make ahead

Arrange cooked drumettes in single layer on baking sheet. Freeze until firm. Transfer frozen drumettes to resealable freezer bag. Freeze for up to 1 month. Just before serving, reheat frozen drumettes on greased baking sheet with sides or in greased casserole in 350°F (175°C) oven for 15 to 20 minutes until heated through.

Parmesan Chicken Wings

Grated Parmesan cheese	1 cup	250 mL
Parsley flakes	1 tsp.	5 mL
Paprika	1 tsp.	5 mL
Salt	1 tsp.	5 mL
Pepper	1/4 tsp.	1 mL
Garlic powder	1/4 tsp.	1 mL
Chicken drumettes (or whole chicken wings, split in half and tips discarded; see Chicken Wing Tips, page 76)	2 lbs.	900 g
Hard margarine (or butter), melted	1/2 cup	125 mL

(continued on next page)

Put first 6 ingredients into small bowl. Mix well.

Dip each drumette into margarine. Dip into cheese mixture until coated. Arrange in single layer on greased foil-lined baking sheet with sides. Bake in 350°F (175°C) oven for about 45 minutes until tender and no longer pink inside. Makes about 16 drumettes or 24 wing pieces.

1 drumette: 166 Calories; 13.9 g Total Fat (6.8 g Mono, 1.9 g Poly, 4.2 g Sat); 33 mg Cholesterol; trace Carbohydrate; trace Fibre; 10 g Protein; 369 mg Sodium

Pictured on page 78/79.

Sweet And Sour Wings

Destined to be the hit of the party.

Chicken drumettes (or whole chicken wings, split in half and tips discarded; see Chicken Wing Tips, page 76)	3 lbs.	1.4 kg
Salt, sprinkle		
Pepper, sprinkle		
Brown sugar, packed	1 cup	250 mL
All-purpose flour	1/4 cup	60 mL
Water	1/2 cup	125 mL
White vinegar	1/4 cup	60 mL
Soy sauce	1/4 cup	60 mL
Ketchup	1 tbsp.	15 mL

Arrange drumettes in single layer on greased foil-lined baking sheet with sides. Sprinkle with salt and pepper. Bake in 350°F (175°C) oven for 30 minutes.

Put brown sugar and flour into small saucepan. Stir. Add water, vinegar, soy sauce and ketchup. Heat and stir on medium until boiling and thickened. Remove from heat. Brush drumettes liberally with sauce. Bake for about 20 minutes, turning and brushing with sauce at least 2 more times, until tender and no longer pink inside. Makes about 24 drumettes or 36 wing pieces.

1 drumette: 126 Calories; 5.9 g Total Fat (2.3 g Mono, 7.5 g Poly, 1.7 g Sat); 28 mg Cholesterol; 11 g Carbohydrate; 1 g Fibre; 43 g Protein; 222 mg Sodium

Pictured on page 78/79.

make ahead

Arrange partially cooked drumettes in single layer on baking sheet. Freeze until firm. Transfer frozen drumettes to resealable freezer bag. Freeze for up to 1 month. Just before serving, arrange thawed drumettes on greased, foil-lined baking sheet with sides. Finish baking as directed in recipe.

These are so light and delicious—one will never be enough!

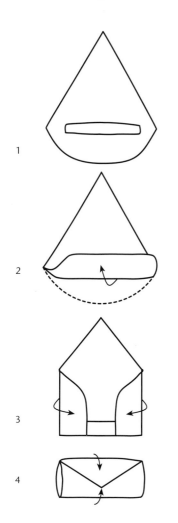

Shrimp Salad Wraps

Short grain white rice	3/4 cup	175 mL
Water	1 1/2 cups	375 mL
Rice vinegar	1 tbsp.	15 mL
Salt	1 tsp.	5 mL
Water	1/4 cup	60 mL
Low-fat vegetable or chicken bouillon cube	1/2	1/2
Garlic clove, minced (or 1/4 tsp., 1 mL, powder)	1	1
Raw medium shrimp, peeled and deveined	48	48
Curry paste (available in Asian section of grocery store)	2 tbsp.	30 mL
Rice paper rounds (9 inch, 22 cm, diameter)	12	12
English cucumber (with peel), quartered lengthwise and cut julienne into 2 inch (5 cm) strips	1/4	1/4
Green onions, sliced lengthwise into 2 inch (5 cm) slivers	2	2
Medium carrot, cut julienne into 2 inch (5 cm) strips	1	1

CHILI DIPPING SAUCE		
Chili sauce	1/4 cup	60 mL
Low-sodium soy sauce	2 tbsp.	30 mL
Rice vinegar	2 tbsp.	30 mL
Prepared horseradish	1 tsp.	5 mL
Liquid concentrated beef flavouring (such as Bovril)	1 tsp.	5 mL

Dried crushed chilies, sprinkle

Combine first 4 ingredients in medium saucepan. Bring to a boil on medium. Reduce heat to medium-low. Cover. Simmer for 20 minutes until water is absorbed and rice is tender. Set aside to cool.

(continued on next page)

Heat second amount of water and partial bouillon cube in large frying pan on medium. Add garlic. Cook until garlic softened.

Add shrimp. Stir-fry for about 3 minutes until shrimp are pink. Do not drain any remaining broth. Remove shrimp to paper towels. Cool shrimp enough to handle. Slice in half lengthwise. Return to frying pan.

Add curry paste. Stir-fry for 1 minute.

Soak rice paper rounds, 1 at a time, in shallow pan of hot water for about 1 minute until soft. Cut into quarters. Divide cucumber, green onion and carrot evenly for 48 wraps. 1. Place vegetables crosswise along wide end of rice paper wedges. Spread 1 tbsp. (15 mL) rice on top of vegetables. Top each with 2 shrimp halves. 2. Fold rounded end up and over filling. 3. Bring two sides of wrapper over shrimp. 4. Roll up, starting at wide end.

Chili Dipping Sauce: Combine first 5 ingredients in small bowl.

Sprinkle with chilies. Makes about 6 tbsp. (100 mL) sauce. Serve with wraps. Makes 48 salad wraps.

1 salad wrap with 1/2 tsp. (2 mL) sauce: 31 Calories; 0.6 g Total Fat (0.1 g Mono, 0.1 g Poly, trace Sat); 8 mg Cholesterol; 5 g Carbohydrate; trace Fibre; 2 g Protein; 158 mg Sodium

Pictured below.

serving suggestion

Serve chilled, at room temperature, or steamed over boiling water until warm.

These are crispy on the outside and soft on the inside.

make ahead

Freeze unbaked rolls on baking sheet until firm. Transfer frozen rolls to resealable freezer bag. Just before serving, thaw and bake as directed. To bake from frozen state, add an additional 2 minutes to baking time.

serving suggestion

Serve as is or with cocktail picks.

Cheese Bites

Hard margarine (or butter), softened	2 tbsp.	30 mL
Light salad dressing (or mayonnaise)	2 tbsp.	30 mL
Grated sharp Cheddar cheese	3/4 cup	175 mL
Finely diced onion	2 tbsp.	30 mL
Finely chopped pimiento	1 1/2 tsp.	7 mL
Cayenne pepper, sprinkle		
White sandwich bread slices, crusts removed	8	8

Paprika, sprinkle (optional)

Put first 6 ingredients into small bowl. Mix well.

Flatten bread slices with rolling pin. Spread each bread slice with about 1 tbsp. (15 mL) cheese mixture. Roll up, jelly roll-style.

Sprinkle each roll with paprika. Place on ungreased baking sheet. Bake in 350°F (175°C) oven for about 10 minutes until toasted. Cut each roll into 4 pieces. Makes 32 appetizers.

1 appetizer: 38 Calories; 2.1 g Total Fat (1 g Mono, 0.2 g Poly, 0.8 g Sat); 3 mg Cholesterol; 3 g Carbohydrate; trace Fibre; 1 g Protein; 65 mg Sodium

Pictured below.

Coconut Shrimp

Raw large shrimp (about 40 – 60 with tails intact), peeled and deveined	2 1/4 lbs.	1 kg
Large eggs	3	3
Water	1 tbsp.	15 mL
All-purpose flour	1/2 cup	125 mL
Medium unsweetened coconut	3 1/2 cups	875 mL

Cooking oil, for deep-frying

Cut shrimp down back, almost but not through, to other side. Press to flatten slightly.

Beat eggs and water together with fork in small bowl. Dredge shrimp with flour. Dip shrimp into egg mixture. Dip into coconut.

Deep-fry, in batches, in hot (375°F, 190°C) cooking oil for 1 to 2 minutes until golden. Remove to paper towels to drain. Makes about 40 appetizers.

1 appetizer: 107 Calories; 8.4 g Total Fat (1.8 g Mono, 0.9 g Poly, 5.1 g Sat); 45 mg Cholesterol; 4 g Carbohydrate; trace Fibre; 5 g Protein; 36 mg Sodium

Pictured below.

You'll earn rave reviews with these crunchy shrimp appetizers!

serving suggestion

Serve with a sweet chili sauce.

Crisp lettuce leaves encase a soft filling. This is an unusual but very delicious treat.

Lettuce Wraps

Cooking oil	1 tsp.	5 mL
Boneless, skinless chicken breast half (about 1), diced into 1/2 inch (12 mm) pieces	4 oz.	113 g
Grated carrot	1/4 cup	60 mL
Slivered onion	1/4 cup	60 mL
Slivered green pepper	1 tbsp.	15 mL
Slivered red pepper	1 tbsp.	15 mL
Slivered orange pepper	1 tbsp.	15 mL
Water	1/4 cup	60 mL
Package of instant noodles with chicken-flavoured packet, broken into 6 pieces and seasoning packet reserved	3 1/2 oz.	100 g
Unsalted peanuts	1/4 cup	60 mL
Reserved seasoning packet	1/2	1/2
Hoisin sauce	1 tbsp.	15 mL
Liquid honey	1 tsp.	5 mL
Pepper	1/8 tsp.	0.5 mL
Chili powder	1/16 tsp.	0.5 mL
Garlic powder	1/16 tsp.	0.5 mL
Hot pepper sauce	1/4 tsp.	1 mL
Leaf (or butter) lettuce leaves	8	8

Heat cooking oil in large frying pan on medium. Add chicken. Scramble-fry until no longer pink.

Add carrot, onion and peppers. Stir-fry until vegetables are tender-crisp.

Add water and noodles. Stir. Cover. Simmer for about 2 minutes until noodles are softened.

Add next 8 ingredients. Stir until heated through. Transfer to small bowl.

Set bowl on platter and surround with lettuce leaves. Have each person spoon about 1/8 of chicken mixture onto lettuce leaf. Roll. Makes about 8 wraps.

1 wrap: 103 Calories; 3.4 g Total Fat (1.6 g Mono, 1.1 g Poly, 0.5 g Sat); 8 mg Cholesterol; 12 g Carbohydrate; 1 g Fibre; 6 g Protein; 140 mg Sodium

Pictured on page 87.

A bit more time is needed to make these, but it's worth it. Once you get the hang of folding these, assembly will be faster.

serving suggestion

Serve with Spicy Dipping Sauce, page 16, or Soy Fire Dip, page 28.

Spring Rolls

Lean ground chicken	1/2 lb.	225 g
Chopped fresh white mushrooms	1 1/2 cups	375 mL
Sesame (or cooking) oil	2 tsp.	10 mL
Salt	1 tsp.	5 mL
Granulated sugar	1 tsp.	5 mL
Ground ginger	1 tsp.	5 mL
Garlic powder	1/4 tsp.	1 mL
Chopped fresh bean sprouts	3 cups	750 mL
Grated carrot	1/2 cup	125 mL
Green onions, thinly sliced	4	4
Oyster sauce	2 tbsp.	30 mL
Dry sherry	1 tbsp.	15 mL
Egg roll wrappers	25	25
Cooking oil, for deep-frying		

Scramble-fry ground chicken and mushrooms in sesame oil in frying pan until chicken is no longer pink and liquid is evaporated.

Add salt, sugar, ginger and garlic. Stir.

Add bean sprouts, carrot and green onion. Stir-fry on medium-high for about 5 minutes until liquid is evaporated.

Stir in oyster sauce and sherry. Stir-fry for 1 minute.

1. Place 2 tbsp. (30 mL) filling on each wrapper, diagonally off centre, closer to 1 corner. 2. Fold point up and over filling. Dampen open edges with water. 3. Fold side points in over filling. 4. Roll to opposite corner. Press to seal.

Deep-fry, in batches, in hot (375°F, 190°C) cooking oil for about 5 minutes until golden. Remove to paper towels to drain. Makes 25 spring rolls.

1 spring roll: 85 Calories; 1.9 g Total Fat (0.9 g Mono, 0.5 g Poly, 0.2 g Sat); 8 mg Cholesterol; 12 g Carbohydrate; 1 g Fibre; 4 g Protein; 336 mg Sodium

Pictured on page 89.

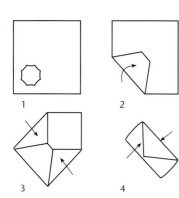

Sesame Pork Balls

Lean ground pork	1 lb.	454 g
Large egg, fork-beaten	1	1
Fine dry bread crumbs	1/2 cup	125 mL
Garlic cloves, minced (or 1/2 tsp., 2 mL, powder)	2	2
Sliced green onion	1/3 cup	75 mL
Low-sodium soy sauce	1 tbsp.	15 mL
Cayenne pepper	1/4 tsp.	1 mL
Salt	1/2 tsp.	2 mL
Pepper, sprinkle		
Sesame seeds	1/2 cup	125 mL
Bamboo skewers (4 inch, 10 cm, length), soaked in water for 10 minutes	24	24

Combine first 9 ingredients in medium bowl until well mixed. Shape into 24 balls, about 1 inch (2.5 cm) in diameter.

Roll balls in sesame seeds.

Preheat lightly greased electric grill for 5 minutes. Push 1 ball onto each skewer. Cook for 10 to 15 minutes, turning often, until no longer pink inside. Makes 24 skewers.

1 skewer: 53 Calories; 3.1 g Total Fat (1.2 g Mono, 1 g Poly, 0.7 g Sat); 15 mg Cholesterol; 2 g Carbohydrate; trace Fibre; 4 g Protein; 111 mg Sodium

Pictured below.

This is a unique way to make pork balls. The sesame seeds are an attractive addition.

make ahead

Assemble pork balls in morning. Chill until ready to bake. Just before serving, bake as directed.

Top Right: Spring Rolls, page 88
Bottom Left: Sesame Pork Balls, this page

A great blend of flavours with a fresh Mediterranean feel.

make ahead

Make filling the day before and chill. Just before serving, spread on bread. Bake as directed.

Bruschetta

Salad dressing (or mayonnaise)	1/2 cup	125 mL
Grated mozzarella cheese	1 cup	250 mL
Medium tomatoes, seeded and finely diced	2	2
Chopped pitted ripe olives	1/4 cup	60 mL
Grated fresh Parmesan cheese (or 2 tbsp., 30 mL, dry)	1/4 cup	60 mL
Dried whole oregano	1 tsp.	5 mL
Dried sweet basil	1/4 tsp.	1 mL
Pepper	1/2 tsp.	2 mL
Baguette bread loaf (about 24 – 27 inches, 60 – 67.5 cm, long)	1	1
Hard margarine (or butter), softened	1/3 cup	75 mL

Combine first 8 ingredients in small bowl.

Cut baguette into 1 inch (2.5 cm) slices. Divide and spread margarine on 1 side of each slice. Place, buttered-side up, on ungreased baking sheet. Divide and spread tomato mixture on bread slices. Bake in 350°F (175°C) oven for about 15 minutes until hot and cheese is melted. Serve warm. Makes about 24 appetizers.

1 appetizer: 99 Calories; 7.1 g Total Fat (3.8 g Mono, 1.2 g Poly, 1.7 g Sat); 6 mg Cholesterol; 6 g Carbohydrate; trace Fibre; 2 g Protein; 170 mg Sodium

Pictured on page 91.

This colourful flatbread is the perfect appetizer after a day of being outdoors. A crisp, golden crust is topped with a delicious mix of fresh ingredients. Enjoy!

Cornmeal Flatbread With Spinach And Onions

All-purpose flour	1 1/3 cups	325 mL
Yellow cornmeal	2/3 cup	150 mL
Instant yeast (1/4 oz., 8 g, envelope)	2 1/4 tsp.	11 mL
Salt	1 tsp.	5 mL
Granulated sugar	1 tsp.	5 mL
Hot water	3/4 cup	175 mL
Olive (or cooking) oil	1 tbsp.	15 mL
Olive (or cooking) oil	1 tbsp.	15 mL
Medium onions, thinly sliced	2	2
Garlic cloves, minced (or 1/2 tsp., 2 mL, powder)	2	2
Paprika	1 tsp.	5 mL
Spinach leaves	2 cups	500 mL
Dark raisins	1/3 cup	75 mL
Slivered almonds	1/3 cup	75 mL
Balsamic (or red wine) vinegar	1 tbsp.	15 mL
Brown sugar, packed	2 tsp.	10 mL
Salt	1/2 tsp.	2 mL
Yellow cornmeal	1 1/2 tsp.	7 mL
Crumbled feta cheese (about 1/2 cup, 125 mL)	2 1/2 oz.	70 g

Combine first 5 ingredients in large bowl.

Add hot water and first amount of olive oil. Mix until stiff dough forms, adding more flour as needed. Turn out onto lightly floured surface. Knead for 1 to 2 minutes until well combined. Place dough on greased baking sheet. Cover with second greased baking sheet. Let stand in oven with light on and door closed for about 30 minutes until puffy.

Heat second amount of olive oil in large frying pan on medium-low. Add onion, garlic and paprika. Cook for about 15 minutes, stirring occasionally, until onion is very soft.

(continued on next page)

Add next 6 ingredients. Heat and stir for about 2 minutes until spinach is wilted. Drain any liquid from frying pan. Set aside.

Roll out dough on lightly floured surface to 10 x 15 inch (25 x 38 cm) rectangle. Sprinkle greased 11 x 17 inch (28 x 43 cm) baking sheet with second amount of cornmeal. Place rectangle on cornmeal. Fold edges of dough up about 1/2 inch (12 mm) to form rim. Spread spinach mixture evenly on dough. Sprinkle with feta cheese. Bake in 450°F (230°C) oven for about 25 minutes until bottom of crust is crisp and browned. Remove to wire rack to cool. Cuts into 12 pieces.

1 piece: 175 Calories; 6.1 g Total Fat (3.4 g Mono, 0.8 g Poly, 1.6 g Sat); 6 mg Cholesterol; 26 g Carbohydrate; 2 g Fibre; 5 g Protein; 383 mg Sodium

Pictured below.

These are every bit as good as they look.

note

Beef is easier to slice when partially frozen.

make ahead

Assemble and broil skewers until beef is medium-rare. Cool. Store in refrigerator until just before serving. Arrange in single layer on greased baking sheet. Bake in 400°F (205°C) oven for about 5 minutes until hot.

serving suggestion

Serve with Red Sweet Sauce, page 95.

Polynesian Satay

Soy sauce	3/4 cup	175 mL
Brown sugar, packed	1/2 cup	125 mL
Cooking oil	2 tbsp.	30 mL
Garlic clove, minced (or 1/4 tsp., 1 mL, powder)	1	1
Ground ginger	1/2 tsp.	2 mL
Thick sirloin steak, cut across grain into 1/8 inch (3 mm) thick slices (see Note, this page)	1 1/2 lbs.	680 g
Bamboo skewers (8 inch, 20 cm, length), soaked in water for 10 minutes	12	12

Combine first 5 ingredients in medium bowl.

Add beef. Stir until coated. Cover. Marinate in refrigerator for at least 30 minutes. Drain and discard marinade.

Thread beef, accordion-style, onto skewers. Place on ungreased baking sheet. Broil on top rack for about 2 minutes per side until desired doneness. Serves 12.

1 serving: 127 Calories; 6.2 g Total Fat (2.8 g Mono, 0.5 g Poly, 2.1 g Sat); 28 mg Cholesterol; 6 g Carbohydrate; 0 g Fibre; 12 g Protein; 578 mg Sodium

Pictured on page 95.

Red Sweet Sauce

Chili sauce	1 cup	250 mL
Fancy (mild) molasses	1/4 cup	60 mL
White vinegar	1/4 cup	60 mL

Combine all 3 ingredients in small saucepan. Heat and stir on medium until heated through. Makes 1 1/2 cups (375 mL).

1 tbsp. (15 mL): 22 Calories; 0.2 g Total Fat (trace Mono, 0 g Poly, trace Sat); 0 mg Cholesterol; 5 g Carbohydrate; 1 g Fibre; trace Protein; 156 mg Sodium

Pictured below.

This yummy sauce requires only three ingredients.

serving suggestion

Pour over hot Polynesian Satay, page 94, or beside as a dip.

Left: Red Sweet Sauce, this page
Right: Polynesian Satay, page 94

The sauce is a perfect complement to the meatballs.

make ahead

Arrange cooked meatballs in single layer on baking sheet. Freeze until firm. Transfer frozen meatballs to resealable freezer bag. Freeze for up to 3 months. Just before serving, reheat frozen meatballs on greased baking sheet with sides or in greased casserole in 350°F (175°C) oven for 15 to 20 minutes until heated through. Add sauce as directed in recipe.

Meatballs With Chutney Sauce

Cooking oil	2 tsp.	10 mL
Chopped onion	1/2 cup	125 mL
Garlic cloves, minced (or 1/2 tsp., 2 mL, powder)	2	2
Finely grated peeled gingerroot	1 tsp.	5 mL
Lean ground chicken	1 lb.	454 g
Fresh bread crumbs (about 4 slices)	1 1/2 cups	375 mL
Large egg	1	1
Chopped fresh parsley (or 1 tbsp., 15 mL, flakes)	1/4 cup	60 mL
Hoisin sauce	2 tbsp.	30 mL
Salt	1/2 tsp.	2 mL
Cayenne pepper	1/8 tsp.	0.5 mL
Coarsely ground pepper	1/16 tsp.	0.5 mL
CHUTNEY SAUCE		
Spicy mango (or other fruit) chutney	1 cup	250 mL
Water	1/2 cup	125 mL
Low-sodium soy sauce	1/3 cup	75 mL
Chili sauce	1 tbsp.	15 mL
Worcestershire sauce	1 tsp.	5 mL
Finely grated peeled gingerroot	1 tsp.	5 mL

Heat cooking oil in small frying pan on medium. Add onion, garlic and ginger. Cook for about 5 minutes until onion is softened and golden. Transfer to medium bowl. Cool to room temperature.

Add next 8 ingredients to onion mixture. Mix well until mixture sticks together when squeezed. Shape into 1 inch (2.5 cm) balls. (See Meatball Tips, page 72.) Arrange in single layer on greased baking sheet. Bake on centre rack in 400°F (205°C) oven for about 10 minutes until no longer pink inside. Remove to paper towels to drain. Transfer to serving bowl. Makes about 45 meatballs.

Chutney Sauce: Process all 6 ingredients in food processor or blender until smooth. Transfer to medium saucepan. Bring to a boil on medium, stirring constantly. Reduce heat to medium-low. Simmer, uncovered, for 5 minutes. Makes 1 1/3 cups (325 mL) sauce. Pour over meatballs.

1 meatball (with sauce): 48 Calories; 1.9 g Total Fat (0.2 g Mono, 0.1 g Poly, 0.1 g Sat); 5 mg Cholesterol; 5 g Carbohydrate; trace Fibre; 3 g Protein; 157 mg Sodium

Pictured on this page.

Baby Cheddar Tarts

CREAM CHEESE PASTRY

Hard margarine (or butter), softened	1/2 cup	125 mL
Block of cream cheese, softened	4 oz.	125 g
All-purpose flour	1 cup	250 mL

FILLING

Grated medium Cheddar cheese	1 cup	250 mL
Large egg	1	1
Milk	1/2 cup	125 mL
Onion salt	1/4 tsp.	1 mL
Salt	1/4 tsp.	1 mL

Cream Cheese Pastry: Beat margarine and cream cheese in medium bowl until smooth and light.

Add flour. Mix well. Roll into long thin log. Cut into 24 slices. Press into small tart pans to form shells.

Filling: Divide Cheddar cheese evenly among tart shells.

Beat egg in small bowl until frothy. Add milk, onion salt and salt. Mix well. Divide and spoon over cheese. Bake in 350°F (175°C) oven for 20 to 25 minutes until set. Makes 24 tarts.

1 tart: 100 Calories; 7.8 g Total Fat (3.7 g Mono, 0.6 g Poly, 3.1 g Sat); 20 mg Cholesterol; 5 g Carbohydrate; trace Fibre; 3 g Protein; 136 mg Sodium

Pictured on page 99 and on back cover.

Your guests will not be able to resist these savoury snacks.

time saver

Measure all 5 filling ingredients (including the Cheddar cheese) into blender. Process until well combined. Pour into shells.

make ahead

Freeze baked tarts in airtight container for up to 3 months. Just before serving, reheat thawed tarts in 325°F (160°C) oven for 15 to 20 minutes (or 30 to 40 minutes if frozen) until heated through.

baby swiss tarts

Use grated Swiss cheese instead of Cheddar cheese.

This hors d'oeuvre is a favourite! The creamy mushroom flavour is so timeless.

make ahead

Arrange uncut, unbaked rolls in single layer on baking sheet. Freeze until firm. Transfer frozen rolls to resealable freezer bag. Freeze for up to 1 month. Just before serving, cut partially thawed rolls into 3 pieces. Bake as directed.

jiffy mushroom rolls

Divide and spread 1 can (10 oz., 284 mL) undiluted cream of mushroom soup on bread slices. Roll up. Cut into 3 pieces. Wrap each with 1/2 slice of half-cooked bacon. Secure with wooden pick. Broil for about 5 minutes, turning once at halftime, until bacon is crisp. Serve hot.

Pictured on page 99.

Mushroom Rolls

Hard margarine (or butter)	1/4 cup	60 mL
Fresh white mushrooms, chopped	1/2 lb.	225 g
Chopped onion	1/2 cup	125 mL
Block of cream cheese, cut up	8 oz.	250 g
Worcestershire sauce	1/2 tsp.	2 mL
Salt	1/2 tsp.	2 mL
Pepper	1/8 tsp.	0.5 mL
Garlic powder	1/8 tsp.	0.5 mL
White sandwich bread loaf (sliced), crusts removed	1	1
Hard margarine (or butter), melted	1/2 cup	125 mL

Melt first amount of margarine in frying pan on medium. Add mushrooms and onion. Cook for 5 to 10 minutes until onion is softened.

Add next 5 ingredients. Stir until cream cheese is melted. Cool.

Roll bread slices with rolling pin. Divide and spread mushroom mixture on each bread slice. Roll up. Brush with second amount of margarine. Cut each roll into 3 pieces. Arrange in single layer on ungreased baking sheet. Bake in 400°F (205°C) oven for 10 to 15 minutes until toasted. Makes about 48 rolls.

1 roll: 72 Calories; 5.4 g Total Fat (2.8 g Mono, 0.5 g Poly, 1.9 g Sat); 6 mg Cholesterol; 5 g Carbohydrate; trace Fibre; 1 g Protein; 125 mg Sodium

Pictured on page 99.

Top: Baby Cheddar Tarts, page 97
Centre Left: Jiffy Mushroom Rolls, this page
Bottom Right: Mushroom Rolls, above

These soft, tasty meatballs are dressed up with an exceptionally good sauce.

make ahead

Transfer cooked meatballs with sauce to resealable freezer bag. Freeze for up to 3 months. Just before serving, reheat frozen meatballs and sauce in ungreased casserole in 350°F (175°C) oven for 15 to 20 minutes, stirring occasionally, until heated through.

Cranberry Meatballs

Large eggs	2	2
Cornflake crumbs	1 cup	250 mL
Finely chopped onion	1/2 cup	125 mL
Soy sauce	2 tbsp.	30 mL
Parsley flakes	1 tbsp.	15 mL
Salt	2 tsp.	10 mL
Pepper	1/2 tsp.	2 mL
Garlic powder	1/2 tsp.	2 mL
Lean ground beef	2 lbs.	900 g
Can of cranberry sauce	14 oz.	398 mL
Chili sauce	1/2 cup	125 mL
Ketchup	1/2 cup	125 mL
Brown sugar, packed	2 tbsp.	30 mL
White vinegar	1 tbsp.	15 mL

Beat eggs with fork in large bowl.

Add next 7 ingredients. Mix well.

Add ground beef. Mix well. Shape into 1 inch (2.5 cm) balls. (See Meatball Tips, page 72.) Put into ungreased 3 quart (3 L) casserole.

Combine remaining 5 ingredients in small bowl. Pour over meatballs. Bake, uncovered, in 350°F (175°C) oven for about 1 1/2 hours. Makes about 78 meatballs.

1 meatball (with sauce): 47 Calories; 1.9 g Total Fat (0.8 g Mono, 0.1 g Poly, 0.7 g Sat); 12 mg Cholesterol; 5 g Carbohydrate; trace Fibre; 3 g Protein; 167 mg Sodium

Pictured on page 101.

Zucchini Treats

Large eggs, fork-beaten	4	4
Finely chopped onion	1/2 cup	125 mL
Grated Parmesan cheese	1/2 cup	125 mL
Cooking oil	1/2 cup	125 mL
Parsley flakes	1 tsp.	5 mL
Salt	1/2 tsp.	2 mL
Celery salt	1/2 tsp.	2 mL
Dried whole oregano	1/2 tsp.	2 mL
Garlic powder	1/4 tsp.	1 mL
Biscuit mix	1 cup	250 mL
Thinly sliced zucchini (with peel)	3 1/2 cups	875 mL
Grated Parmesan cheese	1/4 cup	60 mL

Put first 9 ingredients into medium bowl. Beat well.

Add biscuit mix and zucchini. Stir well. Turn into greased 9 x 13 inch (22 x 33 cm) pan.

Sprinkle with second amount of Parmesan cheese. Bake in 350°F (175°C) oven for about 30 minutes until browned. Cuts into 54 squares.

1 square: 44 Calories; 3.3 g Total Fat (1.7 g Mono, 0.8 g Poly, 0.6 g Sat); 17 mg Cholesterol; 2 g Carbohydrate; trace Fibre; 1 g Protein; 103 mg Sodium

Pictured below.

You may cut these larger if you prefer. Parmesan cheese gives these little treats a delightful flavour.

make ahead

Bake ahead. Cool completely. Do not cut. Cover and chill for up to 24 hours or freeze for up to 6 months. Remove from refrigerator about 30 minutes before serving. Cut while still cold. Remove from freezer 1 to 2 hours before serving. Cut while still partially frozen.

Top Left: Cranberry Meatballs, page 100
Bottom Right: Zucchini Treats, this page

The contrast between the dark beef and the orange cheese creates an attractive pinwheel effect.

make ahead

Make the rolls the day before. Do not cut. Wrap tightly and chill. Just before serving, slice and secure with wooden picks.

serving suggestion

Serve slightly chilled or at room temperature.

These scrumptious rolls are bursting with flavour. Watch out—they will be gone before you know it!

presentation idea

Cut on the diagonal into 1 1/2 inch (3.8 cm) slices. Secure with cocktail picks.

Beefy Roll-Ups

Block of light cream cheese, softened	4 oz.	125 g
Sour cream	1/4 cup	60 mL
Chopped chives	2 tsp.	10 mL
Prepared horseradish	1 1/2 tsp.	7 mL
Prepared mustard	1 tsp.	5 mL
Flour tortillas (8 inch, 20 cm, diameter)	4	4
Shaved deli roast beef	8 oz.	225 g
Grated medium Cheddar cheese	1 1/4 cups	300 mL

Mix first 5 ingredients well in small bowl.

Divide and spread cream cheese mixture on each tortilla. Lay beef over top. Sprinkle with Cheddar cheese. Roll up tightly. Wrap in plastic wrap. Chill for at least 1 hour. Trim ends. Cut each roll into 10 slices, for a total of 40 slices.

1 slice: 46 Calories; 2.6 g Total Fat (0.8 g Mono, 0.2 g Poly, 1.4 g Sat); 10 mg Cholesterol; 2 g Carbohydrate; trace Fibre; 3 g Protein; 68 mg Sodium

Pictured on page 103.

Curried Chicken Rolls

Chili oil	1 tsp.	5 mL
Boneless, skinless chicken breast halves (about 4), cut lengthwise into long strips	1 lb.	454 g
Salt	1/4 tsp.	1 mL
Pepper	1/8 tsp.	0.5 mL
Curry paste (available in Asian section of grocery store)	1 tbsp.	15 mL
Mango chutney	1 tbsp.	15 mL
Worcestershire sauce	1/4 tsp.	1 mL
English cucumber (with peel)	1	1
Green onions, thinly sliced lengthwise	4	4
Flour tortillas (10 inch, 25 cm, diameter), warmed in oven	4	4
Chopped fresh cilantro (or fresh parsley)	2 tbsp.	30 mL

(continued on next page)

Heat chili oil in frying pan on medium until hot. Add chicken. Sprinkle with salt and pepper. Stir-fry for about 3 minutes until browned.

Stir in curry paste, chutney and Worcestershire sauce. Cook for 10 minutes, stirring often, until chicken is no longer pink inside.

Slice cucumber in half lengthwise. Slice each half lengthwise into 4 strips. Divide and arrange cucumber, green onion and chicken mixture at bottom end of each tortilla.

Sprinkle with cilantro. Roll up tightly, jelly roll-style. Cut into 1 inch (2.5 cm) slices. Secure with wooden picks. Makes 40 chicken rolls.

1 chicken roll: 33 Calories; 0.5 g Total Fat (0.2 g Mono, 0.1 g Poly, 0.1 g Sat); 7 mg Cholesterol; 4 g Carbohydrate; trace Fibre; 3 g Protein; 45 mg Sodium

Pictured below and on back cover.

Left: Beefy Roll-Ups, page 102
Right: Curried Chicken Rolls, page 102

This wonderful appetizer has an irresistible Asian flair.

notes

There are two very different black bean sauce products available with the same name. What we refer to here is a thinner, smoother product that can be used as is. The concentrated version is paste-like and somewhat chunky. Both are found in the Asian section of the grocery store.

To toast sesame seeds, spread evenly in ungreased shallow pan. Bake in 350°F (175°C) oven for 5 to 10 minutes, stirring or shaking often, until desired doneness.

make ahead

Assemble in morning. Cover. Chill until ready to serve. Bake as directed.

Beefy Pepper Dim Sum

Large green pepper	1	1
Large red pepper	1	1
Large yellow pepper	1	1
Lean ground beef	1/2 lb.	225 g
Garlic clove, minced (or 1/4 tsp., 1 mL, powder)	1	1
Salt	1/2 tsp.	2 mL
Chopped green onion	1/4 cup	60 mL
Finely diced water chestnuts	1/4 cup	60 mL
Prepared black bean sauce (see Note, this page) or soy sauce	1 1/2 tbsp.	25 mL
Large egg, fork-beaten	1	1
All-purpose flour	1 tbsp.	15 mL
Sesame seeds, toasted (see Note, this page)	1 tbsp.	15 mL

Cut peppers in half crosswise. Remove seeds and white ribs. Cut each half into 4 pieces, for a total of 24 pieces.

Scramble-fry ground beef, garlic and salt in frying pan on medium-high for about 4 minutes until beef is no longer pink. Remove from heat.

Add next 5 ingredients. Mix well.

Arrange pepper pieces, skin-side down, on lightly greased baking sheet. Divide and spoon beef mixture into pepper pieces. Sprinkle with sesame seeds. Bake in 350°F (175°C) oven for 10 to 15 minutes until peppers are tender-crisp. Makes 24 appetizers.

1 appetizer: 26 Calories; 1.3 g Total Fat (0.5 g Mono, 0.2 g Poly, 0.4 g Sat); 14 mg Cholesterol; 1 g Carbohydrate; trace Fibre; 2 g Protein; 88 mg Sodium

Pictured on page 105 and on back cover.

The savoury mushroom flavour of these tarts will warm you from the inside out.

make ahead

Prepare filling. Cool. Bake tart shells. Cool. Divide filling among tart shells. Freeze in airtight container for up to 3 months. Just before serving, reheat thawed tarts in 325°F (160°C) oven for 15 to 20 minutes (or 30 to 40 minutes if frozen) until heated through.

Mushroom Tarts

Hard margarine (or butter)	1 tbsp.	15 mL
Chopped fresh mushrooms	1 cup	250 mL
Chopped green onion	1 tbsp.	15 mL
All-purpose flour	2 tbsp.	30 mL
Salt	1/4 tsp.	1 mL
Skim evaporated milk (or half-and-half cream)	2/3 cup	150 mL
Frozen mini-tart shells, thawed	18	18

Melt margarine in medium saucepan. Add mushrooms and green onion. Cook for 5 to 10 minutes, stirring often, until mushrooms are golden.

Add flour and salt. Mix well.

Add evaporated milk. Heat and stir until boiling and thickened. Cool. Makes generous 1 cup (250 mL) filling.

Place unfilled tart shells on ungreased baking sheet. Bake in 400°F (205°C) oven for 10 to 13 minutes until lightly browned. Cool. Divide mushroom mixture evenly among tart shells. Bake for about 5 minutes until hot. Remove tarts from foil cups. Makes 18 tarts.

1 tart: 53 Calories; 3 g Total Fat (1.6 g Mono, 0.6 g Poly, 0.7 g Sat); trace Cholesterol; 5 g Carbohydrate; trace Fibre; 1 g Protein; 100 mg Sodium

Pictured on page 107.

The wholesome flavour of the blue cheese and the sweetness of the dates are a perfect combination.

Date And Blue Cheese Tarts

Pastry for 2 crust pie, your own or a mix

Large eggs	2	2
Buttermilk (or reconstituted from powder)	1/3 cup	75 mL
Ground nutmeg	1/2 tsp.	2 mL
Finely chopped dates	1/2 cup	125 mL
Blue cheese, crumbled (about 1/3 cup, 75 mL)	1 1/2 oz.	43 g

(continued on next page)

Roll out pastry on lightly floured surface to 1/4 inch (6 mm) thickness. Cut 24 circles with 3 1/4 inch (8.1 cm) cutter. Press circles into ungreased mini-muffin cups.

Beat eggs, buttermilk and nutmeg in medium bowl.

Add dates and blue cheese. Stir. Fill each tart shell with 2 tsp. (10 mL) date mixture. Bake in 375°F (190°C) oven for about 15 minutes until set. Makes 24 tarts.

1 tart: 79 Calories; 4.5 g Total Fat (2 g Mono, 0.5 g Poly, 1.6 g Sat); 19 mg Cholesterol; 8 g Carbohydrate; trace Fibre; 2 g Protein; 103 mg Sodium

Pictured below.

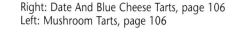

Right: Date And Blue Cheese Tarts, page 106
Left: Mushroom Tarts, page 106

make ahead

Freeze baked tarts in airtight container for up to 3 months. Just before serving, reheat thawed tarts in 325°F (160°C) oven for 15 to 20 minutes (or 30 to 40 minutes if frozen) until heated through.

serving suggestion

Serve either warm or at room temperature.

These tasty wings have an unmistakable zip.

make ahead

Arrange partially cooked drumettes in single layer on baking sheet. Freeze until firm. Transfer frozen drumettes to resealable freezer bag. Freeze for up to 1 month. Just before serving, reheat frozen drumettes on greased baking sheet with sides or in greased casserole in 350°F (175°C) oven for 15 to 20 minutes until heated through.

Glazed Wings

Chicken drumettes (or whole chicken wings, split in half and tips discarded; see Chicken Wing Tips, page 76)	3 lbs.	1.4 kg
Apricot jam	1 cup	250 mL
Apple cider vinegar	3 tbsp.	50 mL
Soy sauce	2 tsp.	10 mL
Onion powder	1/4 tsp.	1 mL
Ground ginger	1/4 tsp.	1 mL

Arrange drumettes in single layer on greased foil-lined baking sheet. Bake in 350°F (175°C) oven for 30 minutes.

Measure remaining 5 ingredients into small saucepan. Heat and stir on medium-low until simmering. Makes about 1 1/4 cups (300 mL) sauce. Brush over drumettes. Bake for 15 to 20 minutes, turning and brushing with sauce 2 or 3 times, until tender and no longer pink inside. Makes about 24 drumettes or 36 wing pieces.

1 drumette (with sauce): 89 Calories; 3.9 g Total Fat (1.6 g Mono, 0.8 g Poly, 1.1 g Sat); 19 mg Cholesterol; 9 g Carbohydrate; 0 g Fibre; 5 g Protein; 53 mg Sodium

Pictured on page 109.

These first-rate chicken wings will marinate as they cook. Delicious!

make ahead

Freeze cooked drumettes, with liquid, for up to 1 month. Just before serving, reheat frozen drumettes in ungreased roaster or casserole in 350°F (175°C) oven for 15 to 20 minutes until heated through.

Oriental Wings

Chicken drumettes (or whole chicken wings, split in half and tips discarded; see Chicken Wing Tips, page 76)	3 lbs.	1.4 kg
Soy sauce	1 cup	250 mL
Water	1/2 cup	125 mL
Granulated sugar	1/2 cup	125 mL
Salt	1/2 tsp.	2 mL
Ground ginger	1/4 tsp.	1 mL
Garlic powder	1/4 tsp.	1 mL

Place drumettes, meaty side down, in large ungreased baking pan or roaster.

(continued on next page)

Mix next 6 ingredients well in small bowl. Pour over drumettes. Bake, uncovered, in 350°F (175°C) oven for 1 1/2 to 2 hours, turning after 45 minutes, until tender and no longer pink inside. Makes about 24 drumettes or 36 wing pieces.

1 drumette (with sauce): 80 Calories; 3.9 g Total Fat (1.6 g Mono, 0.8 g Poly, 1.1 g Sat); 19 mg Cholesterol; 5 g Carbohydrate; 0 g Fibre; 6 g Protein; 793 mg Sodium

Pictured below.

variation

Use an equal amount of liquid honey in place of the sugar.

Top Left: Oriental Wings, page 108
Centre Right: Glazed Wings, page 108
Bottom Left: Yakitori, page 110

These little chicken kabobs are a unique and appealing appetizer. Make plenty.

Yakitori

Soy sauce	3/4 cup	175 mL
Granulated sugar	1/4 cup	60 mL
Cooking oil	1 tbsp.	15 mL
Garlic clove, minced (or 1/4 tsp., 1 mL, powder)	1	1
Ground ginger	1/2 tsp.	2 mL
Boneless, skinless chicken breast halves (about 2), cut into bite-size pieces	8 oz.	225 g
Green onions, cut into 1 inch (2.5 cm) pieces	8	8
Bamboo skewers (4 inch, 10 cm, length), soaked in water for 10 minutes	24	24

Combine first 5 ingredients in medium bowl.

Add chicken and green onion. Cover. Marinate in refrigerator for about 30 minutes. Drain, reserving marinade.

Bring marinade to a boil in small saucepan. Boil for 5 minutes. Thread 2 pieces of chicken and 2 pieces of green onion alternately onto each skewer. Place on broiler rack. Broil on second rack from top for about 3 minutes per side, basting with marinade several times, until chicken is no longer pink inside. Makes 24 kabobs.

1 kabob: 31 Calories; 0.7 g Total Fat (0.4 g Mono, 0.2 g Poly, 0.1 g Sat); 5 mg Cholesterol; 3 g Carbohydrate; trace Fibre; 3 g Protein; 546 mg Sodium

Pictured on page 109.

Quesadilla Starters

Grated Monterey Jack cheese	2 cups	500 mL
Flour tortillas (8 inch, 20 cm, diameter)	6	6
Can of diced green chilies, drained	4 oz.	113 g
Medium avocado, chopped (optional)	1	1
Large tomato, finely diced	1	1
Finely chopped onion	1/3 cup	75 mL
Cooking oil (see Note, this page)	2 tbsp.	30 mL

Scatter 1/3 cup (75 mL) cheese over half of each tortilla.

Divide green chilies, avocado, tomato and onion over cheese. Dampen tortilla edges with water. Fold tortilla over filled half. Press edges with fork to seal. Cover with damp tea towel to prevent drying out.

Heat 1 tbsp. (15 mL) cooking oil in frying pan on medium-low. Cook folded tortillas, in 2 or 3 batches, for about 3 minutes per side until browned and cheese is melted. Cut into 4 wedges each, for a total of 24 wedges.

1 wedge: 92 Calories; 5.6 g Total Fat (2.4 g Mono, 0.7 g Poly, 2.2 g Sat); 9 mg Cholesterol; 7 g Carbohydrate; trace Fibre; 4 g Protein; 89 mg Sodium

Pictured below.

Here's an appetizer that won't crumble when you bite into it. Excellent served hot or cold.

note

You may prefer to lightly grease the frying pan with cooking spray and add only 1 tbsp. (15 mL) cooking oil.

variation

Use cheese and veggies that you have on hand. Prepare, assemble and brown as directed.

After one handful, you'll be hooked on these dark, caramel-flavoured nuts.

Caramelized Nuts

Granulated sugar	1 cup	250 mL
Water	1/2 cup	125 mL
Nuts (your choice)	2 cups	500 mL

Heat sugar in heavy frying pan on medium until melted and caramel in colour.

Stir in water. It will spatter furiously so be careful. Stir constantly until caramel melts and mixes with water. Sugar may lump, but continue stirring and heating until smooth.

Add nuts. Stir until coated. Spread evenly on greased baking sheet with sides. Bake in 300°F (150°C) oven for 30 minutes. Cool. Makes 2 cups (500 mL) nuts.

1/4 cup (60 mL) nuts: 251 Calories; 14.8 g Total Fat (3.4 g Mono, 9.4 g Poly, 1.3 g Sat); 0 mg Cholesterol; 29 g Carbohydrate; 1 g Fibre; 3 g Protein; 3 mg Sodium

Pictured on page 113.

These delicious, crunchy nuts make the perfect gift for a friend or dinner host.

Sugar-Coated Nuts

Mixture of pecan halves, walnut halves and whole blanched almonds	4 cups	1 L
Egg whites (large), room temperature	2	2
Granulated sugar	1 cup	250 mL
Salt	1/16 tsp.	0.5 mL
Hard margarine (or butter), melted	2 tbsp.	30 mL

Spread nuts evenly in ungreased shallow baking pan. Bake in 350°F (175°C) oven for about 10 minutes, stirring or shaking often, until toasted. Cool. Reduce heat to 325°F (160°C).

Beat egg whites in medium bowl until soft peaks form. Gradually beat in sugar and salt until stiff. Fold in cooled nuts.

Grease baking sheet with sides with margarine. Spread nut mixture on baking sheet. Bake for about 30 minutes, stirring every 8 to 10 minutes, until toasted. Makes about 5 1/2 cups (1.4 L) nuts.

1/4 cup (60 mL) nuts: 177 Calories; 14.4 g Total Fat (9 g Mono, 3.4 g Poly, 1.3 g Sat); 0 mg Cholesterol; 13 g Carbohydrate; 1 g Fibre; 2 g Protein; 23 mg Sodium

Pictured on page 113.

Top Right: Sugar-Coated Nuts, above
Bottom Left: Caramelized Nuts, above

A first-course classic!

note

If using small mushrooms, omit mozzarella cheese or place only a few shreds on each cap to prevent cheese from toppling off.

make ahead

Stuff mushrooms in morning. Cover and chill. Just before serving, broil as directed.

Favourite Mushrooms

Fresh large white mushrooms	24	24
Hard margarine (or butter)	3 tbsp.	50 mL
Finely chopped onion	1 cup	250 mL
Lean ground beef	1/4 lb.	113 g
Finely chopped celery	2 tbsp.	30 mL
Ketchup	1/4 cup	60 mL
Fine dry bread crumbs	1/4 cup	60 mL
Garlic powder	1 tsp.	5 mL
Salt	1/2 tsp.	2 mL
Pepper	1/2 tsp.	2 mL
Grated Parmesan cheese	1/4 cup	60 mL
Grated part-skim mozzarella cheese (see Note, this page)	1/2 cup	125 mL

Remove stems from mushrooms. Chop stems finely. Set aside.

Melt margarine in medium frying pan on medium-high. Add onion, ground beef and celery. Scramble-fry until onion is softened and beef is no longer pink.

Add reserved mushroom stems and next 5 ingredients. Stir well. Remove from heat. Divide and stuff filling into mushroom caps. Arrange in single layer on ungreased baking sheet.

Sprinkle with Parmesan cheese and mozzarella cheese. Broil on second rack from top for about 5 minutes until heated through. Serve immediately. Makes 24 stuffed mushrooms.

1 stuffed mushroom: 43 Calories; 2.7 g Total Fat (1.4 g Mono, 0.2 g Poly, 0.8 g Sat); 4 mg Cholesterol; 3 g Carbohydrate; trace Fibre; 2 g Protein; 134 mg Sodium

Pictured on this page.

Shrimp Cocktail

Shredded iceberg lettuce	1 1/2 cups	375 mL
Can of medium shrimp, rinsed and drained	4 oz.	113 g
Peeled and diced cooking apple (such as McIntosh)	1/2 cup	125 mL
Finely chopped celery	1/4 cup	60 mL
Chili sauce	3/4 cup	175 mL
Lemon juice	2 tsp.	10 mL
Worcestershire sauce	1/4 – 1 tsp.	1 – 5 mL
Onion powder	1/2 tsp.	2 mL
Salt	1/4 tsp.	1 mL

Line sherbet glasses with lettuce. Divide shrimp over lettuce, saving a few for garnish if desired.

Combine remaining 7 ingredients in small bowl. Spoon sauce over shrimp. Makes 4 to 5 appetizers.

1 appetizer: 101 Calories; 0.8 g Total Fat (0.1 g Mono, 0.2 g Poly, 0.2 g Sat); 43 mg Cholesterol; 17 g Carbohydrate; 4 g Fibre; 8 g Protein; 929 mg Sodium

Pictured below.

A very special beginning that is fit for a very special meal. This will become a family tradition at your holiday gatherings.

time saver

Use a frozen shrimp ring, thawed, for quick assembly and uniform-sized shrimp.

variation

Omit apple. Double the amount of celery.

Impress your friends and family with this easy Oriental appetizer.

serving suggestion

Serve with Spicy Dipping Sauce, page 16, or Soy Fire Dip, page 28.

Green Onion Cakes

All-purpose flour	2 cups	500 mL
Salt	1/2 tsp.	2 mL
Very hot, but not boiling, water	3/4 cup	175 mL
Thinly sliced green onion	3/4 cup	175 mL
Cooking oil	2 tbsp.	30 mL
Salt, sprinkle		

Measure flour and salt into food processor.

With lid in place and machine running, pour hot water slowly into food chute until dough starts to form a ball. Turn dough out onto lightly floured surface. Knead for about 1 minute until smooth. Cover with plastic wrap. Let stand for at least 30 minutes. Shape into long roll. Divide into 12 portions.

Put green onion into shallow bowl. Flatten 1 piece of dough slightly between your palms. Press each side into green onion. Knead into dough. Shape into flattened circle. Roll out on lightly greased surface with greased rolling pin into 4 1/2 inch (11 cm) circle. Repeat with remaining dough, keeping onion cakes covered with plastic wrap to prevent drying out.

Heat 2 tsp. (10 mL) cooking oil in non-stick frying pan on medium-high. Arrange 4 onion cakes in single layer in frying pan. Cook on both sides, flattening down with lifter, until brown patches appear. Do not overcook. They should be soft, pliable and chewy. Remove to paper towels to drain. Sprinkle with salt. Repeat with remaining cooking oil and onion cakes. Cut into 2 or 4 pieces each. Makes 12 green onion cakes.

1 green onion cake: 103 Calories; 2.5 g Total Fat (1.4 g Mono, 0.8 g Poly, 0.2 g Sat); 0 mg Cholesterol; 17 g Carbohydrate; 1 g Fibre; 2 g Protein; 115 mg Sodium

Pictured on page 117.

Centre Left: Green Onion Cakes, above
Bottom Right: Pot Stickers, page 118

Allow a little extra time to make these—they're worth it! They are visually impressive and so tasty. Your guests will love them.

serving suggestion

Serve with Spicy Dipping Sauce, page 16, or Soy Fire Dip, page 28.

Pot Stickers

Grated cabbage	3/4 cup	175 mL
Lean ground pork	6 oz.	170 g
Cooked shrimp (about 5 oz., 140 g)	3/4 cup	175 mL
Finely chopped green onion	3 tbsp.	50 mL
Soy sauce	1 tbsp.	15 mL
Cornstarch	1 tsp.	5 mL
Ground ginger	1/4 tsp.	1 mL
Garlic powder	1/4 tsp.	1 mL
Salt	1/4 tsp.	1 mL
Dumpling wrappers	36	36
Boiling water	12 cups	3 L
Hard margarine (or butter)	2 tsp.	10 mL

Put first 9 ingredients into medium bowl. Mix well.

Put 2 1/2 tsp. (12 mL) pork mixture onto centre of 1 dumpling wrapper. Dampen edge of wrapper with water. Fold over. Press to seal. Repeat with remaining pork mixture and dumpling wrappers, keeping rolled pot stickers covered with damp tea towel to prevent drying out.

Cook pot stickers, in 3 batches, in boiling water in large uncovered pot or Dutch oven on medium-high for 5 minutes. Remove with slotted spoon. Rinse with cold water.

Melt margarine in non-stick frying pan on medium. Arrange pot stickers close together in frying pan. Cook on 1 side only until well browned. Makes 36 pot stickers.

1 pot sticker: 19 Calories; 0.5 g Total Fat (0.3 g Mono, 0.1 g Poly, 0.1 g Sat); 8 mg Cholesterol; 1 g Carbohydrate; trace Fibre; 2 g Protein; 70 mg Sodium

Pictured on page 117.

Green Chili Snacks

Creamed cottage cheese	1 cup	250 mL
Large eggs	4	4
All-purpose flour	1/3 cup	75 mL
Hard margarine (or butter), softened	3 tbsp.	50 mL
Baking powder	1/2 tsp.	2 mL
Baking soda	1/2 tsp.	2 mL
Salt	1/2 tsp.	2 mL
Grated sharp Cheddar cheese	1 1/2 cups	375 mL
Can of diced green chilies	4 oz.	113 g

Put first 7 ingredients into medium bowl. Beat on medium until mixed.

Add cheese and green chilies. Stir. Turn into greased 8 × 8 inch (20 × 20 cm) baking dish. Bake in 350°F (175°C) oven for 45 to 55 minutes until set and lightly browned on top. Cuts into 25 pieces.

1 piece: 68 Calories; 4.7 g Total Fat (1.9 g Mono, 0.3 g Poly, 2.1 g Sat); 42 mg Cholesterol; 2 g Carbohydrate; trace Fibre; 4 g Protein; 193 mg Sodium

Pictured below.

A simple, delicious recipe that's so easy to prepare.

make ahead

Bake ahead. Cool completely. Do not cut. Cover and chill for up to 24 hours or freeze for up to 6 months. Remove from refrigerator about 30 minutes before serving. Cut while still cold. Remove from freezer 1 to 2 hours before serving. Cut while still partially frozen.

serving suggestion

As an alternative, reheat just before serving in 325°F (160°C) oven for 5 to 10 minutes. Serve warm.

It takes extra time to get this dish into the refrigerator but it's ready to serve with barely any effort. The shrimp taste great as is—no dip is necessary.

serving suggestion

Serve with cocktail picks.

Marinated Shrimp

Bay leaves	3	3
Dried crushed chilies	2 tsp.	10 mL
Whole allspice	1 tsp.	5 mL
Whole cloves	1 tsp.	5 mL
Mustard seed	1 tsp.	5 mL
Whole peppercorns	1 tsp.	5 mL
Boiling water	10 cups	2.5 L
Salt	4 tsp.	20 mL
Raw medium shrimp (about 70 – 80 with tails intact and not peeled)	2 lbs.	900 g
MARINADE		
Water	1/2 cup	125 mL
Cooking oil	1/4 cup	60 mL
White vinegar	1/3 cup	75 mL
Worcestershire sauce	2 tbsp.	30 mL
Prepared mustard	1 tsp.	5 mL
Celery seed	1 tsp.	5 mL
Celery salt	1/2 tsp.	2 mL
Salt	1/2 tsp.	2 mL
Cayenne pepper	1/8 tsp.	0.5 mL
Large onion, thinly sliced	1	1

Tie first 6 ingredients in double layer of cheesecloth.

Add to boiling water and salt in large pot or Dutch oven.

Add shrimp. Return to a boil. Boil, uncovered, for 2 to 3 minutes until shrimp are pink and curled. Drain. Cool. Peel and devein. Discard cheesecloth bag and contents.

Marinade: Combine first 9 ingredients in small bowl.

Layer 1/2 of shrimp in large bowl. Layer 1/2 of onion over shrimp. Layer with remaining shrimp and remaining onion. Pour marinade over all. Cover. Marinate in refrigerator for at least 24 hours. Transfer shrimp, onion and marinade to serving bowl or deep platter. Makes about 75 shrimp.

1 shrimp (with marinade): 20 Calories; 0.9 g Total Fat (0.5 g Mono, 0.3 g Poly, 0.1 g Sat); 24 mg Cholesterol; trace Carbohydrate; trace Fibre; 3 g Protein; 56 mg Sodium

Pictured on page 121.

These succulent meatballs will be a hit every time! Dip in Apricot Sauce.

apricot sauce

In a small bowl combine 1 cup (250 mL) apricot jam, 3 tbsp. (50 mL) cider vinegar and 1/4 tsp. (1 mL) paprika. Stir well, pour into a pretty bowl and dip in.

These are very striking, and they taste even better than they look!

Polynesian Meatballs

Lean ground beef	2 lbs.	900 g
Can of water chestnuts, drained and finely chopped	10 oz.	284 mL
Soy sauce	3 tbsp.	50 mL
Brown (or granulated) sugar, packed	1 tbsp.	15 mL
Garlic cloves, minced	2	2
Parsley flakes	1 tsp.	5 mL
Onion powder	1/2 tsp.	2 mL

Put all 7 ingredients into large bowl. Mix well. Shape into 1 inch (2.5 cm) balls. (See Meatball Tips, page 72.) Place on ungreased baking sheet with sides. Bake in 375°F (190°C) oven for about 15 minutes until meatballs are no longer pink inside. Makes about 78 meatballs.

1 meatball: 20 Calories; 1 g Total Fat (0.4 g Mono, trace Poly, 0.4 g Sat); 6 mg Cholesterol; 1 g Carbohydrate; trace Fibre; 2 g Protein; 45 mg Sodium

Pictured on page 123.

Crab Tartlets

Large eggs	2	2
All-purpose flour	2 tbsp.	30 mL
Salad dressing (or mayonnaise)	1/2 cup	125 mL
Milk	1/2 cup	125 mL
Green onions, finely chopped	3	3
Can of crabmeat, drained and cartilage removed, flaked	4 1/4 oz.	120 g
Grated Swiss cheese	2 cups	500 mL
Frozen mini-tart shells, thawed	60	60

Beat eggs in medium bowl until frothy. Add flour, salad dressing and milk. Stir well. Add green onion, crab and cheese. Stir to combine well.

Place tart shells on ungreased baking sheet. Divide cheese mixture evenly among tart shells. Bake on lowest rack in 350°F (175°C) oven for about 40 minutes until set. Makes 60 tarts.

1 tart: 45 Calories; 3.5 g Total Fat (1.5 g Mono, 0.7 g Poly, 1.1 g Sat); 12 mg Cholesterol; 2 g Carbohydrate; trace Fibre; 2 g Protein; 50 mg Sodium

Pictured on page 123.

Top: Polynesian Meatballs, above
Bottom: Crab Tartlets, above

Throughout this book measurements are given in Conventional and Metric measure. To compensate for differences between the two measurements due to rounding, a full metric measure is not always used. The cup used is the standard 8 fluid ounce. Temperature is given in degrees Fahrenheit and Celsius. Baking pan measurements are in inches and centimetres as well as quarts and litres. An exact metric conversion is given on this page as well as the working equivalent (Metric Standard Measure).

Pans

Conventional – Inches	Metric – Centimetres
8 × 8 inch	20 × 20 cm
9 × 9 inch	22 × 22 cm
9 × 13 inch	22 × 33 cm
10 × 15 inch	25 × 38 cm
11 × 17 inch	28 × 43 cm
8 × 2 inch round	20 × 5 cm
9 × 2 inch round	22 × 5 cm
10 × 4 1/2 inch tube	25 × 11 cm
8 × 4 × 3 inch loaf	20 × 10 × 7.5 cm
9 × 5 × 3 inch loaf	22 × 12.5 × 7.5 cm

Oven Temperatures

Fahrenheit (°F)	Celsius (°C)	Fahrenheit (°F)	Celsius (°C)
175°	80°	350°	175°
200°	95°	375°	190°
225°	110°	400°	205°
250°	120°	425°	220°
275°	140°	450°	230°
300°	150°	475°	240°
325°	160°	500°	260°

Spoons

Conventional Measure	Metric Exact Conversion Millilitre (mL)	Metric Standard Measure Millilitre (mL)
1/8 teaspoon (tsp.)	0.6 mL	0.5 mL
1/4 teaspoon (tsp.)	1.2 mL	1 mL
1/2 teaspoon (tsp.)	2.4 mL	2 mL
1 teaspoon (tsp.)	4.7 mL	5 mL
2 teaspoons (tsp.)	9.4 mL	10 mL
1 tablespoon (tbsp.)	14.2 mL	15 mL

Cups

1/4 cup (4 tbsp.)	56.8 mL	60 mL
1/3 cup (5 1/3 tbsp.)	75.6 mL	75 mL
1/2 cup (8 tbsp.)	113.7 mL	125 mL
2/3 cup (10 2/3 tbsp.)	151.2 mL	150 mL
3/4 cup (12 tbsp.)	170.5 mL	175 mL
1 cup (16 tbsp.)	227.3 mL	250 mL
4 1/2 cups	1022.9 mL	1000 mL(1 L)

Dry Measurements

Conventional Measure Ounces (oz.)	Metric Exact Conversion Grams (g)	Metric Standard Measure Grams (g)
1 oz.	28.3 g	28 g
2 oz.	56.7 g	57 g
3 oz.	85.0 g	85 g
4 oz.	113.4 g	125 g
5 oz.	141.7 g	140 g
6 oz.	170.1 g	170 g
7 oz.	198.4 g	200 g
8 oz.	226.8 g	250 g
16 oz.	453.6 g	500 g
32 oz.	907.2 g	1000 g (1 kg)

Casseroles

Canada & Britain		United States	
Standard Size Casserole	Exact Metric Measure	Standard Size Casserole	Exact Metric Measure
1 qt. (5 cups)	1.13 L	1 qt. (4 cups)	900 mL
1 1/2 qts. (7 1/2 cups)	1.69 L	1 1/2 qts. (6 cups)	1.35 L
2 qts. (10 cups)	2.25 L	2 qts. (8 cups)	1.8 L
2 1/2 qts. (12 1/2 cups)	2.81 L	2 1/2 qts. (10 cups)	2.25 L
3 qts. (15 cups)	3.38 L	3 qts. (12 cups)	2.7 L
4 qts. (20 cups)	4.5 L	4 qts. (16 cups)	3.6 L
5 qts. (25 cups)	5.63 L	5 qts. (20 cups)	4.5 L

tip index

recipe index

most loved recipe collection most loved recipe collection most loved recipe collection
loved recipe collection most loved recipe collection most loved recipe collection most
ction most loved recipe collection most loved recipe collection most loved recipe col
most loved recipe collection most loved recipe collection most loved recipe collection
tion most loved recipe collection most loved recipe collection most loved recipe colle
most loved recipe collection most loved recipe collection most loved recipe collection
e collection most loved recipe collection most loved recipe collection most loved reci
ction most loved recipe collection most loved recipe collection most loved recipe col
most loved recipe collection most loved recipe collection most loved recipe collection
loved recipe collection most loved recipe collection most loved recipe collection most
ction most loved recipe collection most loved recipe collection most loved recipe col
most loved recipe collection most loved recipe collection most loved recipe collection
tion most loved recipe collection most loved recipe collection most loved recipe colle
most loved recipe collection most loved recipe collection most loved recipe collection
e collection most loved recipe collection most loved recipe collection most loved reci
ction most loved recipe collection most loved recipe collection most loved recipe col
most loved recipe collection most loved recipe collection most loved recipe collection
loved recipe collection most loved recipe collection most loved recipe collection most
ction most loved recipe collection most loved recipe collection most loved recipe col
most loved recipe collection most loved recipe collection most loved recipe collection
tion most loved recipe collection most loved recipe collection most loved recipe colle
most loved recipe collection most loved recipe collection most loved recipe collection
e collection most loved recipe collection most loved recipe collection most loved reci
ction most loved recipe collection most loved recipe collection most loved recipe coll
most loved recipe collection most loved recipe collection most loved recipe collection
loved recipe collection most loved recipe collection most loved recipe collection most
ction most loved recipe collection most loved recipe collection most loved recipe col
most loved recipe collection most loved recipe collection most loved recipe collection
tion most loved recipe collection most loved recipe collection most loved recipe colle
most loved recipe collection most loved recipe collection most loved recipe collection
e collection most loved recipe collection most loved recipe collection most loved reci